RADICALLY REPUBLICAN IDEAS

The Missing Roadmap
for the Next 250 Years
of American Prosperity

DAVID SHARPE

Do it for yourself.

Do it for your family.

Do it for your community.

Do it for future generations.

TABLE OF CONTENTS

PART 1

Intro and Background

WHY THIS BOOK EXISTS

For the past 250 years, the United States has stood out as a model of hope, promise, and prosperity. Since the country's founding, generation after generation of Americans have strived toward the goal of a more perfect union. Despite its flaws and challenges, it remains a land where dreams take wing and aspirations are given life. However, the future success and prosperity of its citizens is not guaranteed. In fact, the United States currently faces existential challenges—problems that threaten the very essence of its prosperity. There is still time to address those challenges if we act now—together—with collective action and resolve. This book offers both a roadmap and a blueprint for ensuring American greatness over the next 250 years.

We'll do that by candidly examining the good and bad aspects of where we are today. We'll also provide a holistic assessment of what we all can do to improve the country's prospects at every level: individual, community, cultural, governmental, and on the world stage. We will lay out ideas and solutions to rekindle America's promise.

The stakes are higher than ever, but united in purpose, we can build an America as bright as our boldest dreams. Your future and legacy, your children's futures, and the legacies we leave for generations yet unborn hinge on the choices made today. The time for action is now. Let's get to it.

WHAT'S MISSING?

RADICAL IDEA #1: We need long-term plans.

Effective leaders have a vision for the future and a plan for getting there. They have a practical roadmap and clear strategies that detail how to get from where we are to where we need to be.

Where is the current US administration's long-term plan? What about the candidates for the next US Presidential election or the current administration's most vocal critics—where are their long-term plans? Is their current plan "I'm your least bad option, so put me in power"?

We need smart, actionable long-term plans. As a country, we need to take those plans seriously and execute toward delivering on those visions for our future. In this book we put forth a long-term vision for America, with the intent of rallying millions to work collectively for the benefit of all and of future generations. Short-term concerns matter, but having a long-term strategy and viable roadmap to getting there is vital.

Consider China's five-year plans, which have been instrumental in aligning resources to achieve strategic economic reforms, spurring impressive growth. Singapore transformed from a resource-deficient state to a thriving global nexus, thanks to its carefully crafted masterplans. Germany's unwavering commitment to manufacturing excellence, innovative ecosystems, and vocational training continues to reinforce its economic strength.

America must now ask itself: What audacious, unifying goals should we set for the next two, three, or five decades? What decisive steps can place us on an irreversible trajectory towards these lofty national ambitions?

This book is a practical blueprint for steering America confidently towards a prosperous future. We will be specific, outlining what should comprise America's current long-term plan. We will provide prudent fiscal strategies, focusing on investments that will propel us towards our long-term objectives, ensuring that every dollar spent is a step towards realizing our national vision.

At present, I cannot support establishing anything like a non-partisan Long-Term Planning Commission. While the notion of an apolitical body of experts devising a 50-year plan for America is enticing, the risk of political manipulation is too great in today's climate. Instead, I advocate for existing political entities to step up and forge the way forward. It is my hope that such leadership emerges within my lifetime, before it is too late.

PART 2
American Culture

WHY HAS AMERICA BEEN STRONG AND PROSPEROUS?

Over the past 250 years, a unique convergence of advantages has empowered the United States to become a global superpower. America's extraordinary success story can be traced to several key strengths:

Political Foundations

Constitutional Democracy: The US Constitution established a democratic republican form of government with checks and balances between three branches—legislative, executive, and judicial. This limits the power of any one individual or branch. It enumerates certain guaranteed individual rights and liberties in the Bill of Rights, such as freedom of speech, religion, press, and the right to bear arms. It created a federal system that balances power between the national and state governments. This prevents too much power from accumulating at either level. At its core, the US Constitution provides the foundation of our thriving economy, robust governance, and the liberty and well-being of all Americans. The Constitution's enduring success speaks to the prescient genius and unwavering moral principles of the Framers, who crafted a bold framework that has withstood the test of time.

Rule of Law: Consistent application of laws and a relatively non-corrupt system has given businesses and individuals the confidence to invest and innovate. Democracy and America's legal institutions protected freedoms like speech, property, and contract rights that underpinned prosperity.

Limited Government: The founders established a system of checks and balances and separation of powers that limited government control over the economy and people's lives. This freedom has enabled growth.

Decentralized Federal System: The federal structure allowed states to function as "laboratories of democracy", trying out different policies and solutions.

Economic Factors

Entrepreneurial Spirit: Emphasis on individualism and a capitalist economy encourages entrepreneurship and innovation, rewards hard work, and allocated resources efficiently.

Infrastructure Investments: Visionary initiatives such as the Transcontinental Railroad connected distant frontiers and fueled westward expansion. The ambitious Interstate Highway System transformed mobility and commerce in the 20th century, while expansive postal routes and universal service bound the growing nation together. Rural electrification brought modern conveniences to even the most remote areas. Massive water management projects irrigated croplands and provided drought resilience. Municipal sewer and sanitation systems enabled large cities to thrive. Investments in telecommunications, from the telegraph to the internet, linked Americans across vast distances.

Labor and Immigration: Waves of immigrants over the years have provided essential labor and diverse skills, driving economic growth and cultural dynamism.

Education and Innovation

Education and University System: America's public school system along with its universities helped foster human capital by educating generations, paving the way for economic mobility. The US has been and continues to be a home to leading universities and research institutions, making it a natural hub for innovation and technological advancements.

Patent System: The US patent system, enshrined in the US Constitution, is a pillar of America's success in its support of our relentless inventiveness and spirit of innovation. The patent system plays a vital role in encouraging innovation and entrepreneurship by offering protections for inventors. The patent system creates powerful incentives for pioneers to dream big and bring groundbreaking ideas to fruition. The patent system thus unlocked our creative and entrepreneurial energies, spurring the breakthroughs that catapulted America to economic leadership.

Geographic Advantages

Abundant Natural Resources: Rich in minerals, fertile soil, and other natural resources, America has been primed for industrial and agricultural growth from the start.

Vast Territory: The US encompasses a wide range of topographies and climates, conducive for various types of agriculture, mineral extraction, and human habitation. From its inception, America's large interior with interconnective navigable rivers and access to both the Atlantic and Pacific boosted trade and development.

Protection: Oceans on both the eastern and western borders provides a natural barrier, reducing the threat of invasions and enabling the country to choose its battles more selectively compared to other nations which share multiple borders.

Foreign Policy and Military Strength

Economic and Military Dominance: After World War II, the US emerged as a dominant global economic and military superpower.

Global Trade

The US established an international economic order that facilitated trade, investments, and the opening of new markets.

Financial System

Stable Banking System: A relatively stable financial system (despite periodic crises) encouraged domestic savings and foreign investments.

US Dollar: The dominant role of the US dollar in global finance has given the US significant economic and strategic advantages.

American Culture
Individualism and Self-Reliance: The US cultural emphasis on individual rights, initiative, and autonomy has fostered an entrepreneurial spirit and encouraged people to pursue personal achievements, innovations, and entrepreneurship. This, coupled with a work ethic that values hard work, diligence, and success, powers the economy.

The American Dream: The belief in upward mobility—that regardless of one's background, one can achieve success through hard work—has been a motivating factor for both citizens and immigrants.

Meritocracy: The belief that success should be based on merit, not class or status. This provides social mobility.

Pragmatism: The practical, solution-oriented mindset. This has fostered progress and problem-solving.

Optimism: The prevailing attitude of hope, confidence, and determination to succeed. This cultivates resilience.

Freedom of Expression: First Amendment rights have fostered a vibrant culture of debate, art, journalism, and academia. The ability to challenge the status quo often leads to progress and innovation.

Creativity: The promotion of original thought and creative expression. This advances arts, science, and technology.

Community and Volunteerism: There's a strong tradition of community involvement and volunteerism in the US Local communities often come together to support schools, public works, and charitable causes.

Philanthropy: The spirit of charity and use of private wealth for public benefit. This funds education, arts, etc.

Optimism and Resilience: Historically, Americans have exhibited a sense of optimism about the future and a resilience in the face of challenges. This forward-looking perspective has often translated into proactive efforts to adapt and innovate.

Melting Pot Ethos: The US has been a destination for immigrants, leading to a fusion of different cultures, ideas, and traditions. This diversity has been a source of innovation, resilience, and dynamism.

Civic Engagement: While it has varied over time, there's a tradition of civic engagement in the US, where citizens get involved in the democratic process, pushing for reforms and changes as needed.

Future Orientation: The tendency to look forward, plan ahead, think big. This drives progress.

Informality: The casual, informal social style that downplays hierarchy. This enables openness.

WHAT'S GONE WRONG?

Though we face challenges on many fronts, I believe our society and culture need to improve in three key areas: a growing polarization of society, a deep lack of trust in news media, and a lack of a strategy and long-term plan.

The American public and political system have become deeply polarized. Many feel that traditional values are under threat. Millions of other people feel left behind economically and in terms of opportunity. In politics, bipartisan compromise has become increasingly rare as tribalism rises. This gridlock undermines solving big challenges.

RADICAL IDEA #2: Assess people individually, not by groups.

Assessing a whole society and culture as whole is a complex, multi-faceted issue, but I put forward that judging people one by one—assessing each person's character and actions individually—is vastly superior and more productive than judging them by groupings like political affiliation, race, religion, and sex. However, know that you yourself will be often judged by race, religion, age, sex, despite laws or cultural norms to the contrary.

Declining confidence in government, media, science, and other institutions has resulted in a loss of social cohesion. This distrust undermines the role these institutions play in informing and guiding society.

WHAT WENT WRONG WITH THE NEWS INDUSTRY?

RADICAL IDEA #3: The Golden Age of Lying must end.

The current deluge of disinformation and "fake news" needs to be brought to an end.

How did it come to this? The news industry has been profoundly disrupted by the internet age. Traditional journalism's business models have collapsed as audiences migrated online, decimating newspapers' revenues. This financial strain triggered waves of newsroom layoffs, draining journalistic talent and institutional knowledge. The remaining skeletal staffs often lack resources for in-depth reporting or fact-checking.

In this turbulent and unfavorable environment, outlets found that content provoking outrage, fear, or hate attracted the most clicks and shares. This generated short-term profits but corroded public discourse. Nuance was sacrificed for sensational headlines. Facts bent to inflammatory narratives designed to confirm biases rather than inform debate.

The decline of local news has also dealt a blow, removing essential watchdog journalism over key institutions.

RADICAL IDEA #4: Raise the cost of lying in news and politics.

While some steps like fact-checking initiatives and promoting media literacy will help, we cannot rely on the public alone to fix a broken system. Publishers and platforms must reform how news content is produced, optimized, and monetized to realign incentives with quality journalism. Policymakers also have a role in shaping regulations and exploring new economic models to fund public interest reporting.

That all sounds great, but current market forces aren't solving this problem. It seems to be worsening, so tougher steps might be needed.

For example, if a politician lies, enable the power of news organizations and the internet to expose them for doing so. Politicians, like the rest of us, should feel that the truth itself should both sound like and be a good thing. They should not be able to stand behind libel and slander law when they are knowingly and purposefully lying. More aggressive reforms may be needed, consistent with First Amendment rights. For instance, stricter libel laws could deter blatant falsehoods from politicians and other public figures.

HOW TO FIX THE NEWS

RADICAL IDEA #5: Renew journalism's ethos of truth-telling.

Restoring trust in the media is crucial for a functioning democracy. This requires re-anchoring our information ecosystems to journalistic values of truth, accuracy, and transparency rather than chasing clicks at civilization's expense.

Subscriptions and paywalls appear to be a sustainable route for news organizations to fund quality journalism, and they deserve promotion and support. However, the current prevailing distrust toward some news entities has left many reluctant to spend even a penny on such services.

To rebuild trust so that news organizations can survive and thrive in a free market, maybe we should consider some sort of credibility ranking or badging system for both entities and some individuals. Then consumers of information can filter by that criteria to see the news they want to see. Rating systems could help consumers identify verified, principled news sources, if carefully designed to avoid censorship.

Above all, we must renew journalism's ethos of truth-telling. Lying for profit or political gain should be taboo rather than rewarded. Facts and accuracy should be sacrosanct, not optional. News organizations, not the public, bear the primary duty of ensuring the veracity of the information they disseminate. Furthermore, our information ecosystems must reflect democratic ideals of transparency, integrity, and an informed populace. This transformation requires moral clarity from all who shape public discourse.

SOCIAL MEDIA

The rise of social media has enabled misinformation and conspiracy theories to rush into this void. Fabrications multiply unchecked across filter bubbles. Social media incentivizes inflammatory content through algorithms optimized for engagement. This amplifies partisan extremism within echo chambers where users reinforce shared biases. The anonymity of online interactions also breeds aggressive and dishonest discourse. This enables misinformation and fake news to spread rapidly online without any fact checking or editorial oversight.

Foreign influence campaigns have weaponized these vulnerabilities by spreading disinformation aimed at sowing societal division, especially during critical moments like elections.

THE CURRENT RIFT IN AMERICAN SOCIETY

Anyone who has chosen to read this book likely recognizes and shares concerns about the evident divide in American society today. This divide is hard to miss. However, I believe that both sides of this divide share many of the same concerns about the present and their families' futures. I believe that most Americans are good people at heart. I believe this holds true across much of the world as well.

I see the current societal split in American society as a 10-80-10 problem, instead of 50-50. By 10-80-10, I mean 10% of the population of the US is so rigidly far right, they will never change their minds. Another 10% of the population is so far left, they will similarly never budge in their opinions. In this book, we are speaking to that 80% in the middle, and it will take future generations to work toward 5-90-5 or better.

If you are thinking that the middle 80% straddles both major political parties, you are correct, and that is very much by design. Call this approach whatever you like: new republicanism, next-gen GOP, or next-gen Democratic party. I am a passionate independent thinker trying to lead us from where we are to where we should be for the long-term well-being of the country and its citizens.

THE VALUES WE SHARE

RADICAL IDEA #6: The American public has more similarities in its values and dreams than differences.

Charting the commonalities reveals more shared goals than stark differences.

What Americans don't want:
- A government without strategic planning across key areas like the economy, infrastructure, and education.
- Petty, unproductive squabbles.

- Spiraling national debt.
- Forewarnings about the insolvency of social security, Medicare, and Medicaid, with no solutions in sight.

What Americans do desire:
- A functioning and efficient government.
- Representatives who remain in DC, addressing critical issues, rather than frequent fundraising trips.
- Judicious use of tax dollars and government resources.

RADICAL IDEA #7: Nobody good wants to be US President. We need to change that.

Nobody good wants to be US president or in Congress. With rare exceptions, the prevailing political climate deters qualified, ethical individuals from seeking the US presidency or a seat in Congress. This dysfunction in modern politics repels ethical, talented leaders from public service at all levels. We need to seed that field of future leaders by the millions, and not wait for that one person to come along, the one who is willing to deal with the intense problems—for themselves and their family—of being a US political leader in the current toxic climate. I contend that the only way we'll get a truly great, world class leader to emerge for the Presidency in America is if a catastrophe happens first and they feel compelled to step forward.

PRIMING THE LEADERSHIP TALENT PUMP

RADICAL IDEA #8: Increase the pool of future leaders by the millions.

My proposal for cultural overhaul here is to develop and grow future generations of excellent leaders by the millions. In politics, this goal helps us break the current cycle of choosing the least bad option in every election. How? We do this by establishing a solid foundation from which millions can emerge as leaders, all rooted in our fundamental guiding principles

Our Guiding Principles

Our framework for improving American society and culture, person by person, is based on guiding principles rather than inflexible rules or commandments. Guiding principles are fundamental to living a life of excellence. They provide a dynamic yet robust framework for ethical behavior, clear decision making, resilience, personal growth, and fulfillment. They serve as the bedrock of an individual's identity. The goal is to give individuals new options to consider for incorporation into how they choose to live.

Looking more broadly, if millions of people choose the path of excellence now and in coming generations, that will uplift communities and societies as whole worldwide. We will have an ever-growing number of solidly grounded people in all walks of life—a pool from which better leaders can naturally emerge to guide and change the world for the better, a stronger and more enduring engine of innovation and prosperity, and a strengthening of the concepts of family and community around the globe.

This book is about improving the big picture and shaping a better future, which hinges on the collective actions of many. We require an ever-flowing stream of good people, but what exactly constitutes 'good'?

Our 10 Guiding Principles for individuals are:

---

1. Be the gold standard

2. Your happiness is vital

3. Maintain your physical and mental health

4. Continuous self-improvement

5. Stack at least three wins per day

6. Be bold, yet respectful

7. Credibility is your stock in trade

8. Keep your trusted circle tight

9. Spread kindness, goodness, and joy

10. Remember why you live this way

---

1. BE THE GOLD STANDARD.

RADICAL IDEA #9: Be the gold standard of excellent character—always in all ways.

Be a model of impeccable character for your children, your family, your community, and everyone around you.

Excellent character refers to your possession and consistent demonstration of virtuous qualities and moral integrity. It includes honesty, responsibility, respect, kindness, and other values broadly deemed admirable by societies around the world. Someone with excellent character is trustworthy and dependable, consistently making ethical decisions and acting with empathy and consideration towards others.

Someone aiming to embody the gold standard of character avoids actions they would feel ashamed to see as headline news or have discovered by family. It means adhering to one's principles and doing the right thing, even when no one is watching. Upholding excellence of character requires considering how choices would appear if publicly revealed and letting that insight strengthen resolve for integrity. Though maintaining impeccable conduct is challenging, the rewards are great: a clear conscience, self-respect, and trusted influence. We must have the courage and discipline to make decisions we can proudly stand by whether in public or private, simply because they are right.

2. YOUR HAPPINESS IS VITAL.

Your happiness is vital, as it profoundly impacts your whole life and all those around you. When you are happy, you flourish and spread positivity. You become a force uplifting your family, community, and environment. Your whole system of achieving and sustaining excellence suffers if you are unhappy.

Although what you do is for the benefit of others—your family and close friends, your community, and others—don't live your life in misery to achieve that.

Relationships: Happiness has a positive impact on relationships, as it promotes empathy, trust, and stronger connections with others. When you are happy, you are more likely to be supportive and understanding in your interactions, which can contribute to more meaningful and fulfilling relationships.

RADICAL IDEA #10: Treat everyone with respect in your personal life, in politics, in business, and in policy.

Productivity: Happy people tend to be more productive and successful in their professional or business lives. When you are happy, you are more focused, creative, and motivated to achieve your goals.

Social Impact: Your happiness can have a ripple effect on those around you. When you are happy, you are more likely to spread positivity and inspire others to adopt a more optimistic outlook.

Personal Growth: Happiness can foster personal growth by encouraging you to pursue your passions, learn new skills, and engage in activities that enrich your life. A positive mindset can help you overcome obstacles and embrace new challenges, leading to self-improvement and growth.

Resilience: Happy individuals tend to be more resilient in the face of adversity. A positive outlook helps you to bounce back more quickly from setbacks and to find solutions to problems more effectively.

3. MAINTAIN YOUR PHYSICAL AND MENTAL HEALTH.
Your physical and mental health are essential aspects of your overall well-being, as they directly impact your ability to lead a fulfilling, productive, and happy life. The whole system around you is impacted if you are unwell.

Quality of Life: Good physical and mental health enhances your overall quality of life. It allows you to engage in daily activities, maintain social connections, and pursue your passions without being hindered by illness or emotional distress.

Longevity: Maintaining good physical health helps increase your lifespan by reducing the risk of chronic diseases, such as heart disease, diabetes, and obesity. Similarly, good mental health can contribute to a longer life by decreasing the risk of stress-related illnesses and promoting healthy coping mechanisms.

Relationships: Physical and mental health can significantly influence your relationships with others. Good health enables you to be more present, empathetic, and supportive in your interactions, fostering stronger connections with friends, family, and romantic partners.

Productivity: Good physical health provides the energy and stamina needed to accomplish daily tasks and responsibilities, while good mental health supports focus, creativity, and problem-solving abilities. Both are essential for success in personal and professional endeavors.

Emotional well-being: Mental health is closely linked to your emotional well-being. When you take care of your mental health, you are better equipped to manage stress, maintain emotional balance, and develop resilience in the face of adversity.

Prevention of illnesses: Taking care of your physical and mental health can help prevent the onset of various illnesses and conditions. A balanced diet, regular exercise, and stress management techniques contribute to a robust immune system and lower the risk of developing chronic diseases.

Coping skills: Good mental health allows you to develop effective coping skills to navigate life's challenges and setbacks.

This resilience helps maintain emotional stability and promotes personal growth during difficult times.

Positive impact on others: When you prioritize your physical and mental health, you set a positive example for those around you, inspiring them to prioritize their own well-being. This can create a ripple effect of improved health and happiness in your community.

4. CONTINUOUS SELF-IMPROVEMENT.

Learn everything you can about your business, profession, and passions every day. Seize every opportunity that comes near you that you assess will have some type of positive outcome. When your boss, business partner, or clients present a challenge or task, let "yes" be your default response. Make "yes" your approach, and watch your skills, expertise, confidence, credibility, and money pile up.

More broadly, continuous self-improvement is a process of regularly striving for personal growth and development, whether it's in terms of personal or business goals, education, physical health, mental well-being, or personal relationships.

RADICAL IDEA #11: Continuous improvement has its merits personally, in business, in your career, and as a leader.

Skill Enhancement: Continuous self-improvement often involves learning new skills or enhancing existing ones, which can lead to better job prospects, career advancement or business performance. It keeps you competitive in a rapidly evolving world.

Adaptability: The world around us is constantly changing. Through continuous self-improvement, you foster adaptability and resilience, helping you adjust to new environments, challenges, and technologies.

Personal Fulfillment: Self-improvement can lead to personal satisfaction and happiness. Achieving goals you've set for yourself and stacking your daily wins can boost your self-esteem and confidence, leading to an overall better quality of life.

Mental Health: Self-improvement often involves developing better coping mechanisms and emotional intelligence, which can improve mental health. It can help manage stress, depression, and anxiety, leading to better mental and emotional well-being.

Lifelong Learning: The pursuit of self-improvement fosters a love for lifelong learning. This can keep you mentally stimulated and can lead to a more enriched and fulfilled life.

Relationship Improvement: Self-improvement can lead to better interpersonal relationships. By improving communication skills, emotional intelligence, and empathy, we can better connect with and understand others.

Health and Wellness: Often, self-improvement involves adopting healthier lifestyle choices. This can lead to better physical health and longevity, as well as improved mental health.

Personal Growth: Continuous self-improvement encourages personal growth and self-awareness. Understanding our own strengths, weaknesses, passions, and fears is an important part of personal development.

Empowerment: Self-improvement can lead to a sense of empowerment. By setting and achieving personal goals, we can gain a sense of control over our lives.

Legacy: Through continuous self-improvement, you're not only enhancing your life but also potentially making a positive impact on the lives of others, leaving a meaningful legacy.

5. STACK AT LEAST THREE WINS PER DAY.

Strive to have at least three accomplishments per day, every day—with no days off. They don't have to be huge leaps forward or fully completed projects. It's fine if they are just small steps toward your goals. If you haven't stacked at least three wins for today, keep going until you do.

Hard work creates opportunities. Sustained levels of hard work compound over time, yielding significant results. If you consistently act on what needs to be done, whether you feel like it or not, success is far more likely.

Three wins a day might not sounds like much, but it's about 90 a month, which means over 1,000 per year.

A thousand wins per year! Imagine what you can get done toward your goals sustaining that pace.

RADICAL IDEA #12: Did you get your three wins for today?

The benefits are manifold:

Achievement of Goals: Hard work is often necessary to accomplish personal and professional goals. By putting in the effort, you are more likely to achieve the desired outcomes and experience a sense of fulfillment.

Skill Development: Working hard allows you to develop and refine your skills, whether they are related to your job, hobbies, or personal interests. Mastery of these skills can lead to increased confidence and competence.

Professional Success: Employers and colleagues tend to value hard-working individuals who demonstrate dedication and commitment to their work. This can lead to promotions, salary increases, and greater job satisfaction.

Personal Growth: Hard work helps you push beyond your comfort zone, overcome challenges, and grow as a person. This personal growth can contribute to increased self-awareness, resilience, and adaptability.

Discipline and Work Ethic: Developing a strong work ethic through hard work can lead to self-discipline and the ability to manage time and resources effectively. These qualities are valuable in both personal and professional settings.

Builds Character: Hard work helps to build character traits such as perseverance, determination, and resilience. These traits can be beneficial in navigating the ups and downs of life and overcoming obstacles.

Respect and Recognition: People who consistently work hard tend to earn the respect and recognition of others. This can improve your relationships and reputation within your personal and professional networks.

Financial Stability: Working hard can lead to financial rewards and stability, which can contribute to a higher quality of life and greater peace of mind.

Sets an Example: Demonstrating a strong work ethic and commitment to hard work can inspire and motivate others to do the same, leading to a positive ripple effect in your community.

Sense of Accomplishment: Hard work often leads to a sense of accomplishment and satisfaction in knowing that you have given your best effort. This can contribute to improved self-esteem and overall well-being.

6. BE BOLD, YET RESPECTFUL.

RADICAL IDEA #13: You need to be bold, but respect people at all levels.

Many problems and conflicts in life boil down to people not respecting one another. Those could be interpersonal conflicts all the way up to conflicts between nations and civilizations.

As an individual, be bold, get things done, achieve your goals, thrive, prosper, build wealth, take care of the people you care about, and live your life to the fullest, but do so without leaving a trail of damage and broken relationships behind you. Act with confidence and energy, rooted in your values and beliefs, but always with a foundation of respect, considering the feelings, rights, and perspectives of others.

Remember, even in the face of disrespect, hold firm to this principle.

7. CREDIBILITY IS YOUR STOCK IN TRADE.

RADICAL IDEA #14: Your credibility is your stock in trade.

Credibility is how trusted, believable, and convincing you are. Your credibility is your stock in trade. That is true at work, in business, with your family and friends, and in society at large. Think of your credibility as a bank account balance—its value can rise or fall. Once you have lost all credibility, you are diminished in the minds of the particular audience involved. It is sometimes possible to rebuild lost credibility, but it can be a long and difficult process.

It can take years to build your reputation and credibility, and only seconds to lose it all. Don't say or do anything you will regret or be ashamed of—bearing in mind that act could escape notice now and surface years later in front of your family, friends, and business associates. Exercise caution and mindfulness in your actions and words, avoiding impulsive behaviors or statements that could later cause remorse, embarrassment, or damage to yourself or others. It's essential to think before you act and consider both the immediate and the long-term consequences of your decisions.

8. KEEP YOUR TRUSTED CIRCLE TIGHT.

RADICAL IDEA #15: Be careful who you trust.

Keeping your trusted circle tight means surrounding yourself with a small group of people whom you trust and value for their loyalty, honesty, and support. Restricting yourself to a tight-knit trusted circle has several advantages:

Emotional Support: A close group of trusted friends or family members can provide emotional support during difficult times, helping you cope with stress, loss, and other challenges. They can be a reliable source of comfort and encouragement.

Honest Feedback: People in your trusted circle are more likely to provide honest, constructive feedback and advice, helping you grow and improve in various aspects of your life. They are invested in your well-being and personal development, which allows for open communication and genuine guidance.

Stronger Relationships: By focusing on a smaller group of trusted individuals, you can invest more time and energy into deepening those relationships. This can lead to stronger connections and more meaningful interactions.

Reliability: A tightly knit trusted circle is more likely to be there for you when you need them, as they have a vested interest in your well-being and happiness. You can rely on them for help, advice, and support in various situations.

Reduced drama and negativity: By limiting your trusted circle to a small number of close friends and family members, you can minimize exposure to unnecessary drama and negativity, which can be draining and harmful to your mental health.

Confidentiality: A smaller circle of trusted people ensures that your personal information and secrets are more likely to remain confidential. This can provide peace of mind and help protect your privacy.

Shared values: A tight-knit circle of trusted individuals often share similar values and priorities, which can contribute to a sense of belonging and mutual understanding.

Quality over quantity: Focusing on a smaller group of trusted friends allows for more meaningful and fulfilling relationships. It emphasizes the importance of quality connections over a large number of superficial friendships.

Positive influence: Surrounding yourself with trustworthy, supportive people can have a positive impact on your behavior, mindset, and overall well-being. They can inspire and motivate you to pursue your goals and maintain a healthy lifestyle.

Personal growth: Your trusted circle can play a significant role in your personal growth and development, as they challenge you, support you, and encourage you to explore new ideas and experiences.

9. SPREAD KINDNESS, GOODNESS, AND JOY.

Don't be so serious all the time. Have fun! It's good for both you and those around you. Kindness, spreading goodness and joy, and having fun are essential aspects of life that contribute to personal and social well-being.

Spreading goodness and joy: By spreading goodness and joy, you can create a positive ripple effect, inspiring others to engage in similar acts of kindness and generosity. This can contribute to a more harmonious, supportive, and compassionate society.

Having fun: Engaging in fun activities and enjoying life promotes a healthy work-life balance, helps relieve stress, and improves overall well-being. Taking time to have fun can also enhance creativity, problem-solving skills, and productivity.

Social connections: Kindness, spreading joy, and having fun can strengthen social connections and help create lasting friendships. These strong social bonds can lead to increased happiness and improved mental health.

Encourages reciprocity: When you demonstrate kindness, spread joy, and have fun with others, it often encourages them to reciprocate, further promoting a positive and supportive environment.

Enriches lives: Kindness, spreading goodness, and having fun contribute to a richer, more meaningful life. By focusing on these aspects, you can cultivate a greater sense of purpose, happiness, and fulfillment.

10. REMEMBER WHY YOU LIVE THIS WAY.

RADICAL IDEA #16: Don't lose sight of your purpose and most important goals.

You aren't doing all of this for yourself. You don't live this way for your own benefit.

While a lifetime of benefits will accrue to you and you will thrive, your way of life, your hard work, and your pursuit of excellence are for the people you care about the most: your family, spouse, children, and friends who are so close, they're just like family. If you don't have a family of your own right now, you're doing this for your future family: your future wife and your unborn children.

They're your first priority. You are the second. In your mind, see their faces when mustering your energy to finish that project, overcome the next obstacle, or when making that next tough decision. Look right through problems and see their faces to find the energy and courage to overcome setbacks and failures. See their faces when things go well, and the rewards start piling up.

As more people live this way, it uplifts families. Families are the building blocks of communities, and communities are what constitute societies. Regardless of what path you choose—be it public service, business, or otherwise—there is a clear line between the high-quality things you are doing to improve as an individual uplifting your family, your community, and society as a whole.

PART 3

The US Economy

RADICAL IDEA #17: The past success of the US economy is no guarantee of future results.

It will be game over for the US economy in the long term if we don't take the corrective actions we need to take soon. We still have time to make the necessary corrections, but we can't wait forever.

The job market is still strong, with unemployment under 4%, near historic lows, but hiring is slowing, and layoffs are rising in some sectors like tech. Wage growth has been stubbornly lagging inflation, causing real wages to decline. Consumers are spending cautiously amid high prices and rising borrowing costs.

Looking at the longer term, the US retains structural advantages that will likely keep growth positive, though more moderate. The economy is globally competitive in areas like technology, financial services, healthcare, and energy. Population growth is higher than in other developed countries. Debt levels are elevated but not yet unsustainable.

However, there are compelling risks. Rising inequality and polarization strain society. Infrastructure and education need investment. Competition from China and other emerging markets grows. Maintaining US dynamism and global leadership is not guaranteed.

Let's take a look at what is happening, and what is needed going forward.

US FEDERAL DEBT LEVEL

RADICAL IDEA #18: We need to get our financial house in order—starting now.

We face pressing challenges—ones that could be catastrophic if neglected. However, they are not insurmountable if we act promptly and decisively.

The most pressing concern facing us is what measures can effectively reduce or eradicate the America's federal debt?

Eliminating the USA's federal debt is a complex challenge due to the size of the debt and the many economic, political, and social factors at play. However, there are several strategies and methods, both on the revenue side and the expenditure side, that could help reduce or eliminate the debt over time.

THE MONEY COMING IN

RADICAL IDEA #19: No tax increases can happen until government spending is firmly brought under control.

Tax Increases: While it may prove to be necessary to raise personal and corporate income tax rates in the long run, we need to be careful not to break the system right now. The amount of waste, fraud, and abuse is too high to accurately assess what the right taxation level should be now or projecting forward. Individuals, families, and businesses do not have the spare capacity to throw more money into the current wasteful and inefficient system. They might find the means if we grow the economy and can show the extra tax revenue is needed to build what we require to thrive in the future. First, though, we must ruthlessly and aggressively drive the wasteful spending out. Our immediate priority should be to decisively eliminate unnecessary spending and redirect available funding as necessary to achieve the goals in our long-term plan.

RADICAL IDEA #20: Substantially raise the annual threshold for when social security contributions are no longer collected per person.

For individuals, social security isn't collected from their pay anymore once they cross $168,600 in earnings in any given year. Americans overwhelmingly support Social Security and are willing to pay more to preserve and improve its benefits. For some immediate support for Social Security, the American public will likely go along with removing the salary threshold of roughly $168,600 for social security contributions, or at least raising it significantly to $400,000 or more.

THE MONEY GOING OUT

RADICAL IDEA #21: Spend money on the right things.

The Federal government needs to spend money, but are we spending money on the right things? Often, the term "right" is left undefined. By "right", I mean "toward hitting our goals in the long-term plan". What I don't mean is wasteful expenditures, undue corporate benefits, or appeasing donors at the expense of collective interests. Of course, hitting goals in a long-term plan requires having a long-term plan. This book outlines a solid foundation for such a long-term plan.

Broaden the Tax Base: Close unintentional loopholes in and simplify the tax code to ensure more consistent revenue collection.

Economic Growth: Policies and investments that stimulate long-term economic growth can increase tax revenues without raising rates.

RADICAL IDEA #22: Don't implement policy that drives money and investment out of the country. It is possible to go too far and break the engine of the economy.

We must avoid alienating existing capital and deterring potential investments through excessive taxation and a business-hostile climate. Such capital is the lifeblood of business startups, driving growth and spurring innovation.

Instead, supporting a thriving startup and entrepreneurial ecosystem is essential for the US economy, fostering job creation, propelling innovation, and enhancing economic resilience. By nurturing this environment, we not only fuel job growth and technological advancement but also attract global talent and address critical societal challenges in health, education, and the environment, ultimately enriching American lives.

DEFICIT SPENDING

RADICAL IDEA #23: Deficit spending is okay if it is aligned with a smart long-term plan.

Deficit spending is sometimes necessary, or even desirable, if it is in support of a carefully thought-out long-term plan. However, America has fallen into a reckless pattern, even in prosperous times, of outlays chronically exceeding revenues.

Unless reversed soon, this trajectory threatens our economic stability. With debt swelling each year, we move closer to a tipping point that would force crippling austerity or monetary disaster.

The prudent path is to purge waste aggressively first: streamline bureaucracy, reshape entitlements, crack down on special interest subsidies—shed every expense not truly serving the common good.

With budgets and long-term planning responsibly aligned, we can rehabilitate revenue structures to sustainably fund strategic investments and a social safety net. Deficits in lean times can prime growth.

We must break the addiction to excess in any climate. Rediscipline in spending coupled with fair tax reforms will restore fiscal health. With balance and moderation, deficits and debt can judiciously energize American society again instead of slowly sinking it.

RADICAL IDEA #24: Don't touch Social Security, Medicare, or Medicaid spending until waste and fraud elimination efforts have completed in each program.

Entitlement Reform: It may later be necessary to modify programs like Social Security, Medicare, and Medicaid to ensure their long-term sustainability, possibly by adjusting age eligibility, benefits, or contribution rates. For now, these programs too must undergo a rigorous mandatory review to eliminate waste, fraud, and abuse. If we still have funding issues for these vital programs that millions of Americans rely upon, then we can consider making any needed adjustments to help ensure they are around to help support future generations of Americans.

Given current challenges like low savings rates and inadequately funded retirement plans affecting millions of citizens of all ages, the significance of these programs is clear. Their potential failure could imperil countless senior citizens. By responsibly reinforcing these crucial safeguards, we uphold our commitment to those who built their futures on the promise of security.

DEFENSE SPENDING

RADICAL IDEA #25: Replace or relaunch the DoD's Fraud, Waste, and Abuse Program.

Spending on defense and the US military is vital and a strategic priority for the foreseeable future. However, we need to continuously evaluate and reduce defense expenditures without compromising national security or America's strategic interests.

While the US Department of Defense's (DoD) Fraud, Waste, and Abuse program has had oversight responsibilities for decades, its execution remains lacking. Egregious waste persists across defense budgets, squandering taxpayer funds.

To curb this, the program needs revitalization—not just consolidation of existing patchwork efforts. Truly eliminating waste requires commitment from the top down to reset cultural norms, take transparency seriously, and enforce accountability at all levels.

DoD leaders must send an unequivocal message: abuse of public dollars will not be tolerated. Back this with sufficient staff resources, internal controls, and inspector general independence. Establish channels for safe whistleblowing and protect those who speak up.

America needs a military capable of meeting complex threats, but sheer spending is no substitute for strategy and discipline. With diligent oversight and a zeal for efficiency, DoD can maintain readiness while becoming a paragon of public stewardship. This will require tenacity in the face of inertia. We owe taxpayers—and troops pledged to defend this nation—no less.

The money this program has historically offered can incentivize people. Pay 10% of the actual, realized savings in a year, with no limit. If it is a billion dollars, pay the billion to the whistleblower.

BUDGET CHALLENGES AS A TOOL

RADICAL IDEA #26: Use budget challenges across the US federal government.

I think many would agree that efforts to eliminate wasteful and inefficient spending across the federal government are worthwhile, but what will work to get that done? How can we identify and cut programs or projects that are inefficient or have outlived their usefulness?

Make annual budget challenges part of a government-wide financial health Get-Well Plan. For example, annually require a 3, 5, or 10% reduction in budgets across government agencies until the waste is driven out. If a leader or department head says they cannot reach the annual budget goal, consider that their resignation notice and replace them with someone who can.

GOVERNMENT SOURCING AND PROCUREMENT

RADICAL IDEA #27: In government sourcing and contracting, disfavor cost-plus terms in favor of fee-for-service.

Generally, fee-for-service models tend to work better in competitive markets, giving providers incentives to maximize efficiency. Cost-plus models can work for specialized services with unpredictable materials or labor needs.

Creating sound, practical sourcing rules across the US government that strongly favor a specific price for services or goods in contract terms rather than cost-plus alone will drive out countless billions of dollars of waste across multiple agencies. There will be years of aggressive pushback from those benefitting from the current arrangements, so appropriate and robust protections for whistleblowers must exist.

US MONETARY POLICY

Positioning the United States for enduring economic strength over the next 20, 50, or even 100 years through monetary policy is a complex endeavor, as it requires foresight into economic trends, technological changes, demographic shifts, and global events that may arise in the future. Overall, the United States has done well managing its unique position in the world economy.

RADICAL IDEA #28: The Federal Reserve System should retain its autonomy.

The United States should have a central bank, and it should remain autonomous. Maintaining the Fed's independence—while enhancing transparency and communication—has been, and will continue to be, crucial in enabling the effective conduct of monetary policy oriented toward economic stability and growth.

Why?

- It isolates monetary policy decisions from short-term political pressures. This allows the Fed to take a longer-term view focused on economic stability rather than political cycles.

- Research shows independent central banks are more effective at managing inflation. Politicians often face incentives to overstimulate the economy to boost their electoral chances, resulting in higher inflation.

- Central bank independence contributes to market stability by committing to a non-political rules-based policy framework. Markets can trust the Fed will follow its mandates rather than partisan aims. In our interconnected global economy, coordination with other central banks and international institutions can help in addressing global challenges and ensuring stability.

- Autonomy gives the Fed credibility in setting interest rates. Rate changes are more impactful when the Fed is seen as non-political and focused on economic objectives.

- Governance stability enables the Fed to be more decisive in responding to financial crises as lender of last resort.

- Periodic congressional oversight and transparency requirements ensure the Fed does not operate in isolation from democratic accountability. Clear communication about monetary policy intentions can help guide market expectations and reduce uncertainty. This involves not just conveying decisions, but also the rationale behind them.

ROLE OF THE US DOLLAR

RADICAL IDEA #29: Maintain the US dollar's place as a reserve currency.

There are several major benefits to the US dollar being the world's leading reserve currency, and our long-range strategy should include maintaining those advantages as long as possible:

- **Cheaper Borrowing:** The strong global demand for US dollars allows the US government and American companies to borrow at lower interest rates. This reduces costs for investments.

- **Enhanced Influence:** Reserve status gives the US added economic and political leverage over international markets and global rules/standards setting.

- **Revenue Gains:** Being the global reserve provides seigniorage revenue as foreigners hold interest-bearing dollars and Treasury bonds. Estimates suggest gains to the US range from $100–200 billion annually.

- **Convenient Exchange Medium:** Having the globally dominant currency makes international trade and finance much simpler for US-based entities, reducing transaction costs.

- **Safety Appeal:** Dollar assets, especially Treasuries, are seen as a safe haven during crises due to the size and strength of US markets. This further bolsters demand.

- **Leverage over Sanctions:** The central role of the dollar in finance and trade allows the US to impose potent sanctions denying access to dollar transactions.

RADICAL IDEA #30: Continue robust support for America's role as a global financial hub.

America's role as a global financial hub provides several important benefits:

- It generates tremendous economic value, high-paying jobs, tax revenues, and prestige for the United States. Financial services like banking, insurance, trading markets, investment funds, and advisory services have grown into a major high-tech industry.

- It gives the US "home field advantage" in access to capital, control over global standards setting, and cross-border transaction capabilities important for all industries.

- The concentration of talent and expertise in US financial markets, along with institutions like the SEC, contributes to efficient capital allocation, market stability, and investor protections.

- Deep, liquid US financial markets allow businesses and governments to easily access financing, hedging mechanisms, and world-class advisory services.

- The US hub attracts tremendous foreign capital to invest in America, enhancing growth and development.

- The innovative and competitive nature of US markets supports the creation of new financial technologies, instruments, and business models.

- US prominence in global finance gives it added influence over economic policies, regulations, and governance standards worldwide.

THE DERIVATIVES MARKET

RADICAL IDEA #31: Put appropriate controls around the degenerate and reckless gambling in the financial derivatives market.

The 2007–2008 financial crisis nearly devastated economies worldwide, not just in the United States. We teetered on the brink of a collapse that could have reshaped Western civilization. A leading contributor to this precarious situation was the unchecked growth and rampant speculation within the global financial derivatives market, which deeply destabilized the global financial system.

While derivatives can help transfer risk, their sheer scale today—with over $630 trillion in notional value outstanding worldwide—poses enormous systemic threats. This enormity enables dangerous levels of leverage, complexity and interconnectedness that jeopardize stability and often benefit financial middlemen more than underlying investors.

Learning from the past, prudent reforms are imperative to increase transparency, improve collateralization, curb reckless speculation and refocus these markets on genuine hedging versus casino-style bets detached from the real economy.

With thoughtful regulation and smarter use of financial innovation, derivatives can play a constructive role in commercial risk management. We must mitigate the dangers posed by largely unregulated activity of unprecedented size. Markets require rules and boundaries in order to thrive and prevent hazardous contagion. As the last crisis demonstrated, unchecked speculation can inflict heavy costs on global prosperity.

Here are some reasons why more stringent controls are needed on financial derivatives trading:

- **Mitigate Systemic Risk:** Unchecked speculation in complex derivatives exacerbated the 2008 financial crisis.

Opaque markets and interconnected counterparty exposures threaten stability.

- **Limit Dangerous Leverage:** High levels of leverage used in many derivative bets multiply both risks and resulting market volatility.

- **Improve Transparency:** More disclosure and reporting rules around derivative positions will shed light on concealed risks.

- **Protect Retail Investors:** Greater oversight is required to clamp down on mis-selling of products like swaps and futures to those who don't understand the risks.

- **Curb Market Manipulation:** More oversight would make it harder for large players to corner, squeeze, or otherwise rig derivatives markets.

- **Ensure Proper Collateralization:** Stricter collateral rules could reduce counterparty default risks and contain damage if a large player fails.

- **Foster Fairer Competition:** Speculative abuses and opacity often benefit large Wall Street institutions over other market participants.

WHAT DOES THIS MEAN FOR ORDINARY PEOPLE?

What does this long-term planning, high-level thinking, and talk about trillions of dollars mean in practical terms for the average American? What among all of that immediately addresses the pervasive sense of hopelessness and their worries about the future and the future of their families that millions of Americans are feeling?

For their day-to-day economic concerns and their concerns about their children's future, this book lays out a practical plan that provides a vision and a promise for the future. What's missing is a sensible and achievable long-term plan for America that lays out what we want to achieve together for the next 5, 10, 20, 50, and 100 years.

With smart long-term planning and execution, we can fuel the economic growth essential to combat stagnant wages and ensure they align with living costs.

With smart long-term planning and execution, we forge clear pathways for those anxious about layoffs, outsourcing, automation, and job stability in the long run.

With smart long-term planning and execution, we rejuvenate industries that are viable and primed to flourish in America.

With smart long-term planning and execution, we can renegotiate trade deals he deemed unfair.

With smart long-term planning and execution, we can **streamline** regulations that stifle entrepreneurship and business growth.

PART 4

The US Political System

THE CONSTITUTION

RADICAL IDEA #32: The US Constitution is the best framework mankind has ever produced for organizing a society and government. Don't let that system break.

The US Constitution is a living testament to the power of democracy, a set of enduring principles that have guided our nation for more than 200 years. It's given us the freedom to speak our minds, the right to assemble, and the power to choose our leaders. The Constitution established critical checks and balances between branches of government and protected the rights of individuals against potential tyranny.

No system of government or founding document is perfect. The Constitution is no exception to that rule. It was written by men of their time, and it reflects the limitations of their understanding. However, it also contains the mechanisms for change, the ability to adapt and evolve to meet the challenges of new generations. However, the American experiment launched in 1787 remains the most successful framework ever conceived for defining a just, free, and prosperous society governed by the rule of law.

The Constitution's inherent balance of idealism and pragmatism is its genius. We must be vigilant against those who would seek to erode its principles or weaken its institutions. We must protect and defend the Constitution so its light may continue guiding the path ahead to form a more perfect union.

CONGRESS'S WORK ETHIC

RADICAL IDEA #33: Members of Congress need to spend more time in D.C. working, than back home fundraising.

Members of Congress should be focused on what matters most: our future. However, they're too distracted by fundraising, partisan gridlock, and the constant need to keep their seats to tackle the challenges facing our country.

Instead of spending 20 hours a week on fundraising calls, begging for millions of dollars from special interests, they should be working on effective solutions.

The two-year election cycle and lack of bipartisanship only make it worse. Members are constantly campaigning, beholden to donors, and unwilling to compromise with the other side. This leaves us with short-term fixes and no long-term vision for our future.

One significant challenge is that representatives no longer spend as much time in the capital as they once did, limiting their opportunities for face-to-face interactions and compromise. This diminishes their ability to effectively represent their constituencies and address pressing issues.

As a start toward improvement, members of Congress should prioritize spending more time in Washington, DC, focusing on legislative duties rather than extensive fundraising activities back in their districts. While fundraising is essential, so is collaboration, forging relationships, and finding common ground with fellow members.

REALIGNING THE MOTIVES OF MEMBERS OF CONGRESS

RADICAL IDEA #34: Implement Warren Buffett's proposal to tie the Congress members' ability to run for office to budget performance.

This proposal isn't mine, but I like it. In a CNBC interview on July 1, 2011, Warren Buffett remarked, *"I could end the deficit in five minutes. You just pass a law that says that any time there's a deficit of more than 3% of GDP, all sitting members of Congress are ineligible for re-election."*

Further elaborating in a New York Times op-ed in August 2011, Buffett wrote:

> *"The reform could be phased in. Current representatives and senators could be exempted from the reform...the prohibition would take effect only after the 2012 election had been held. By then, voters would have had an opportunity to see for themselves how sincerely the incumbents had tackled the deficit problem."*

It's worth noting that Buffett's mention of the 3% deficit benchmark was illustrative rather than a definitive proposal. Nevertheless, the underlying concept—using re-election prospects as an incentive for Congress to maintain fiscal responsibility—holds significant potential.

LEGISLATIVE CLARITY

RADICAL IDEA #35: Congress needs to stop writing vague laws and deferring to the Executive branch to determine what laws actually mean and how to implement them.

Congress has an obligation to enact laws that are clear and well-defined, not vague mandates that lack concrete details and metrics. When legislation is ambiguous or incomplete, it effectively grants the executive branch unchecked power to interpret the law as they see fit. This undermines the separation of powers.

There are a few potential remedies Congress could pursue:

- Require legislative staff to conduct more robust technical review of bills to identify and correct vagueness before passage. Too often, flawed drafting happens due to haste or negligence.

- Institute mandatory independent review panels to assess new legislation for clarity, specificity and enforceability. Feedback would inform revisions.

- Expand subject matter expertise and analytical capacity in Congressional research agencies like CRS (Congressional Research Service) and GAO (Government Accountability Office). If either or both of those support organizations are ineffective, overhaul or replace them. Deep knowledge helps craft detailed laws.

- Increase Congressional oversight over regulatory rulemaking to ensure fidelity to legislative intent. Require periodic review of regulations.

- Limit or end the practice of attaching vague directives in giant omnibus bills that circumvent the typical deliberative process.

In the end, the onus is on Congress to fulfill its duties diligently by enacting laws with sufficient clarity to be properly executed and contain appropriate checks against overreach. While some flexibility in interpretation is needed, excessive vagueness undercuts the role of the people's branch.

THE ZEN OF DRAINING SWAMPS

RADICAL IDEA #36: People of all levels across all branches of the US federal government need to align to and support the nation's long-term plan and strategies. Failure to do so in a timely fashion will be considered a voluntary resignation.

The concept of "draining the swamp" in the 2016 US Presidential election resonated with countless Americans who were disillusioned by the status quo and the direction in which the country seemed to be heading. Yet, where was Trump's comprehensive vision for the future then or now? Has any candidate from either political party presented a concrete, long-term strategy?

This glaring void inspired me to pen this book. We need more than just intentions. We need a well-structured, viable, and thoughtful plan. Our goal is to revitalize the system in a manner that reflects the ideals of the Constitution's Framers yet is attuned to the demands and nuances of the present age.

Simply opposing and critiquing others without a clear roadmap is not a productive approach. The strategies outlined in this book aim to unite Americans under shared goals and aspirations, driving us forward with collective purpose and determination.

PART 5

The US Education System

WHERE ARE WE NOW?

Historically, the US has long prioritized education, with a strong university system that attracts talent from around the world. These institutions have been centers of research, innovation, and thought leadership.

Despite the prestige of its universities, the US does not consistently rank at the top in secondary education outcomes. On the Programme for International Student Assessment (PISA), which evaluates reading, math, and science proficiency, the US regularly trails countries such as Singapore, Japan, and South Korea.

Furthermore, automation and globalization are transforming the workforce, requiring adaptable skills that tests like the PISA cannot measure like critical thinking, problem-solving, and collaboration. The current US system may not adequately equip students for these demands. As a result, the US faces a mismatch between the skills employers need and the skills students possess. This gap could widen if the education system doesn't adapt to evolving workforce needs.

WHERE DO WE NEED TO BE?

RADICAL IDEA #37: The US Department of Education must publish a tactical long-term plan showing how it will overhaul the US education system to align with the US's published long-term strategic plans.

The US Department of Education must publish a tactical long-term plan showing how it will overhaul the US education system, and this tactical plan must align with the US's published strategic long-term plans. Any failure or reluctance to provide such a roadmap by the Department may be seen as an implicit resignation by its top leadership.

The US education system has been criticized in recent years for falling behind other developed countries in terms of student achievement. There are a number of factors that have contributed to this decline, including a lack of funding, teacher shortages, and a focus on standardized testing.

In order to be competitive globally, the US education system needs to make a number of changes. One important change is to increase funding. The US spends less money on education per student than many other developed countries. This lack of funding has led to overcrowded classrooms, outdated textbooks, and a shortage of qualified teachers.

Another important change is to focus on teaching students critical thinking skills. In the economy of the 21st century and beyond, it is more important than ever for students to be able to think critically and solve problems. The current education system is too focused on standardized testing and memorization. Students need to be able to think for themselves and apply what they learn to real-world problems.

The US education system also needs to focus on teaching students creativity and innovation. In the global economy, it is important for students to be able to come up with new ideas and solutions. The current education system is too focused on conformity and obedience. Students need to be encouraged to think outside the box and come up with new and innovative ideas.

Finally, the US education system needs to focus on teaching students how to learn. The pace of change is accelerating. Students need to be able to learn new things quickly and adapt to new situations. The current education system is too focused on teaching specific facts and figures to students. Students need to be taught how to learn on their own and how to apply what they learn to new situations.

Making these changes will not be easy, but it is necessary if the US education system wants to be competitive globally both now and in coming decades.

CREATING A WORLD-CLASS VOCATIONAL EDUCATION SYSTEM

RADICAL IDEA #38: Create a vocational training system as an alternative to college.

Not everyone wants to attend a traditional college. A four-year college degree is not the only route to a rewarding career. As higher education costs continue to rise, we should strengthen alternatives, especially for non-college-bound students.

The US should create a vocational training program similar to what Germany has successfully implemented as an alternate path to college. Germany's renowned vocational education system offers a model the US could emulate to prepare non-college-bound students and revitalize manufacturing. Their programs provide structured on-the-job apprenticeships combined with classroom instruction. Students gain recognized qualifications aligned to employer needs and transition smoothly into well-paid skilled trades and technical roles.

Expanding high-quality vocational training in the US can prepare youth for in-demand jobs without burdensome tuition fees. Modernizing technical education to match Germany's rigorous blend of immersive work experience and class learning could reconnect America's educational pipeline to careers.

Rather than stigmatize vocational paths, we can elevate their prestige. Partnerships between educators and employers can tailor training programs around industry competency standards.

Investing in vocational education ensures all students develop marketable skills matched to growing fields.

College remains an important choice for many. Making technical career training a viable alternative to college creates more opportunities for prosperity.

Some highlights of Germany's vocational program to consider for inclusion in the new US vocational education system include:

- It combines classroom instruction with on-the-job training under the "dual system" model. Students split time between a vocational school and a company.

- Programs typically last 2–3.5 years and focus on career fields like engineering, IT, business, healthcare, skilled trades, hospitality, etc.

- Roughly 50–60% of German high school graduates opt for vocational training instead of university.

- Requirements include having a secondary school diploma and finding a company willing to provide the practical training. Competition can be fierce for top companies.

- The vocational training is regulated by federal law and quality standards. Students must pass exams to graduate and get certified.

- Companies bear the cost of on-the-job training and pay students a monthly salary of 600–850 euros (about 630–880 US dollars) on average.

- Advantages are early focus on a career, earning money, skills development, strong job prospects after graduation. Avoiding university tuition fees and student debt is also a plus.

- Downsides are less flexibility to change careers and limited options for higher level jobs requiring a university degree.

- Unlike in many countries where vocational training may be viewed as a less-desirable alternative, in Germany, vocational training is a highly respected and mainstream choice. Many top business leaders in Germany have come up through the vocational training system.

Germany is not alone in providing accessible vocational training aligned with employer needs. Switzerland and Austria have thriving programs as well. The US should adapt desirable elements of these exemplary models. Customized vocational pathways, designed through coordination between educators and employers, can reinvigorate America's skilled technical workforce. Investing in vocational education ensures students develop in-demand skills matched to new and growing industries.

However, there are some challenges that could make implementing Germany's dual vocational education system difficult in the United States:

- The decentralized education system in the US makes standardized national training and certification problematic. What works in one state may not apply to another.

- Vocational training is traditionally done after high school in the US, while it begins at younger ages in Germany. Adopting the system would require curriculum changes starting as early as middle school.

- America's university culture values academic degrees, while vocational careers are often seen as lesser options. Overcoming this ingrained stigma would be difficult.

- US employers may be reluctant to invest in apprenticeship programs that train students who could then leave for another job. Germany has a more stable workforce.

- Trade unions play a major role in vocational training in Germany. The weaker labor movement in the US makes it difficult to replicate the intimate labor/business collaboration.

- The upfront costs of work-based learning programs can be prohibitive for smaller US employers lacking deep pockets. Cost-sharing models are still emerging.

- State/federal friction on education policy in the US could cause issues trying to implement a unified national vocational training system.

- The German model is designed for a manufacturing-based economy. The US has shifted more towards services, requiring adjustments to vocational programs.

Those challenges are significant, but we as a nation need to overcome them. The US economy needs this support. US businesses need qualified workers. If some parts of the country don't want to participate in the program that is fine, let's develop it where it is welcome and comprehensively address its challenges. With vision, rigor and collaboration, we can clear obstacles and build ladders of opportunity.

SMART INVESTMENTS IN RESEARCH AND DEVELOPMENT

RADICAL IDEA #39: Invest in research and development, especially in areas aligned with the nations long-term plan.

Investing in research and development (R&D) generates substantial economic returns by catalyzing innovation, talent development, and competitive advantage. However, with infinite possibilities but limited resources, determining strategic R&D funding priorities is crucial. How do we invest those limited R&D resources in a manner aligned with and in support of our national long-term plan?

The potential benefits of this more focused and intentional R&D spending are numerous:

- R&D often leads to the development of new technologies, products, and services. Innovations can create new industries or revitalize existing ones, leading to increased economic output.

- Countries that invest in R&D are better positioned to compete in the global market. They are more likely to produce high-value goods and services that can be exported.

- R&D activities can lead to the creation of high-skilled jobs. These jobs often pay higher wages, leading to increased consumer spending.

- A strong commitment to R&D can attract foreign companies to invest in a country, bringing with them capital, technology, and expertise.

- Money spent on R&D tends to circulate within the economy. Salaries paid to researchers, for instance, get spent on goods and services, stimulating other sectors of the economy.

- While the benefits of R&D might not always be immediate, in the long term, countries that invest in research often see sustained economic growth.

- R&D can foster collaboration between public institutions (like universities) and the private sector, leading to the commercialization of research findings.

- Innovations in one industry can benefit others. For example, advancements in materials science can benefit the automotive, aerospace, and construction industries.

- R&D can lead to the development of new tools, technologies, and processes that increase productivity, allowing businesses to produce more with the same resources.

- Countries with diversified economies based on knowledge and innovation are often more resilient during economic downturns.

COLLEGE AFFORDABILITY

RADICAL IDEA #40: Make college more affordable going forward, but do not forgive existing student load debt.

US student loan debt is the massive amount of debt accumulated by millions of Americans who have taken out loans to finance their higher education. As of late 2023, the total outstanding student loan debt in the US has reached $1.7 trillion with more than 43 million borrowers, making it the second-largest type of consumer debt in the country, after mortgages.

The ramifications of this debt are profound and far-reaching. Graduates grapple with the heavy load, which constrains their financial freedom, delaying pivotal life milestones like home ownership, marriage, and family planning. The ripple effects extend to retirement savings and entrepreneurial aspirations, as the weight of debt limits future financial possibilities.

With all empathy for people's challenges in life, it is simply unfair for others to have to pay for their educations. What happened to personal responsibility and integrity? They agreed to take on the debt for their education, and they need to pay their debts. Will people who worked hard and paid off student debt be reimbursed? Will families who sacrificed to pay for their children's education be reimbursed? No? Then, the right path forward is to say no to student debt cancellation.

However, the skyrocketing cost of a college education needs to be brought under control. The escalating expenses call into question the economic viability of investing in a college education, necessitating a critical examination of the value proposition of higher education.

RESPONSIBLE RISK-TAKING

RADICAL IDEA #41: Support a culture of responsible risk-taking.

To maintain the type of competitive edge necessary to be successful going forward, the US needs to encourage and sustain a culture of responsible risk-taking. The US has done well leading the way in some key areas, like the recent remarkable breakthroughs in artificial intelligence. But why has NASA not been able to get astronauts to the space station? SpaceX has to do that.

A culture of responsible risk-taking in an economy involves fostering an environment where individuals and organizations understand, manage, and take risks in a knowledgeable and confident manner. This culture encompasses the values, beliefs, knowledge, attitudes, and understanding of risk shared by a group of people with a common purpose. To balance entrepreneurship support, risk, rewards, innovation, and the prosperity of the citizenry, it is essential to promote a culture that allows and encourages individuals and organizations to take risks in an educated and confident manner.

By promoting a culture of responsible risk-taking, it is possible to strike a balance between supporting entrepreneurship, managing risk, reaping rewards, fostering innovation, and ensuring the prosperity of the citizenry.

ARTIFICIAL INTELLIGENCE—NOW AND LATER

RADICAL IDEA #42: Harvest the value and benefits of artificial intelligence.

Embrace artificial intelligence (AI). The best way for individuals to think about the current state of AI is your job will not be taken by AI. Your job will be taken by another person using AI. AI is a rapidly changing field. It has the potential to automate certain tasks, create new jobs, and increase productivity, ultimately reshaping the future of work. We need to stay on top of what it is good for at any point in time, and what it isn't. This might change in the future, but for now, think of AI as enhancing the workforce, not replacing it.

From a policy perspective, think of it like this: AI currently excels at computationally intensive data processing and pattern recognition, enabling heightened personalization, prediction, optimization, and automation across finance, healthcare, transportation, and various services. Leaders who strategically deploy AI and reskill staff to complement strengths over simply cutting costs can responsibly boost productivity. Consider safe use of AI across all levels of government to improve productivity, improve the quality of government services, and to drive cost out.

PART 6

Our Infrastructure

AN HONEST ASSESSMENT OF US INFRASTRUCTURE

Sound infrastructure is key to our success. How is the US doing overall in the areas of infrastructure?

According to the World Economic Forum's Global Competitiveness Report 2023, the US ranks 13th in overall infrastructure quality, falling behind countries like Singapore (1st), Netherlands (2nd), and Japan (3rd). The American Society of Civil Engineers (ASCE) gives the US's overall infrastructure a grade of C–, highlighting significant room for improvement.

Specific Areas of Strength and Weakness:

- **Transportation:** The US has a vast road network and some of the busiest airports in the world. However, many roads and bridges are in poor condition, and traffic congestion is a major problem in many cities.

- **Energy:** The US has a diverse energy mix, but its energy infrastructure is aging and needs significant upgrades to meet future needs and address climate change concerns.

- **Water and Sanitation:** While most Americans have access to clean water and sanitation, there are significant disparities in service quality and affordability across different regions and income groups.

- **Telecommunications:** The US has a well-developed telecommunications infrastructure, but there are significant gaps in access to high-speed internet in rural and low-income areas.

Challenges and Opportunities:

- **Funding:** The US faces significant funding challenges in maintaining and upgrading its infrastructure. Public investment in infrastructure has declined in recent decades, while the cost of maintaining existing infrastructure has risen.

- **Innovation:** The US needs to invest in innovative technologies and solutions to address infrastructure challenges. This includes areas like renewable energy, smart grids, and sustainable transportation.

- **Environmental Change:** More extreme weather events can damage infrastructure and disrupt services. The US needs to invest infrastructure solutions that are more resilient in the face of extreme weather.

WHERE DO WE NEED TO BE?

Global leaders like Singapore and the Netherlands offer models for strategic infrastructure investment and governance through rigorous long-term planning. Their long-term master plans provide continuity across political cycles.

America should adapt these best practices, laying out a nationwide infrastructure revitalization blueprint aligned to our strategic plans.

Carefully planned and calibrated new infrastructure expenditures—likely reaching trillions of dollars across transport, digital, energy, and water systems—can boost productivity and opportunity when allocated prudently. Robust accountability mechanisms, spending trackers and progress metrics will ensure transparency while demonstrating returns on these vital investments.

HOW DO WE GET THERE?

BROADBAND

For the United States to effectively enhance its broadband infrastructure for the next century, the US must consider the following strategies:

- **Fiber Infrastructure:** Fiber broadband is recognized as a crucial component that adds to local GDP, increases home values, and creates high-paying jobs. It has both immediate and long-lasting impacts on communities and offers unlimited capacity, making it the preferred choice for long-term infrastructure investment.

- **Technology Neutrality:** While there is debate about technology neutrality—allowing local and state governments to choose their infrastructure—there is a strong argument for prioritizing fiber due to its capability to support future demands like telehealth, precision farming, smart homes, 8K streaming, and AI-driven applications.

- **Speed Requirements:** There's a challenge in defining what "minimally acceptable speeds" are. As the demands for bandwidth increase, especially in rural areas, the US should aim for higher than the minimum to prevent a growing digital divide and to ensure that rural citizens have access to the highest quality broadband.

- **Long-Term Economic Growth:** Any new broadband infrastructure should aim to facilitate sustainable, long-term economic growth and improved health and education outcomes. This requires not only connecting individuals but also empowering local communities with the digital skills they need to thrive in an increasingly online world.

- **Effective Partnerships:** The success of broadband expansion depends on partnerships with clear intentions. State broadband officials should collaborate with local champions to identify common problems and promote shared goals.

- **Oversight and Accountability:** There needs to be oversight in the distribution of funds allocated for broadband expansion to ensure that the money is spent effectively and that no region is left behind.

- **Preparing for Future Demands:** Studies have shown that a household's bandwidth requirements are set to increase dramatically in the coming years. This underscores the need for infrastructure that can support this growth, with fiber being the only technology capable of meeting such demands.

ROADS AND TRANSPORTATION SYSTEM

Taking the long view on policy and infrastructure lifecycle economics is vital. The investments made today will serve coming generations. Maintaining the road and transportation systems is expensive. By planning ambitiously, deploying innovation and ensuring equitable access, transportation networks can responsibly evolve for and support national needs 100 years or more hence.

Here are some key things the US should focus on regarding road and transportation infrastructure over the next century:

- Increase investment in public transit infrastructure like high-speed rail to provide efficient low carbon alternatives to highways as population growth continues.

- Expand adoption of smart infrastructure technologies like AI-optimized traffic signals to dynamically manage transportation network capacity.

- Overhaul infrastructure funding model by transitioning from gasoline tax to usage-based vehicle mileage fees to account for more efficient electric vehicles.

- Convert select highways into protected digital infrastructure corridors to facilitate deployment of electric vehicle charging stations, broadband fiber routes, among other uses.

- Utilize advanced materials like durable polymer concretes in road and bridge construction to reduce maintenance costs over decades-long lifespans.

- Subsidize municipal projects revitalizing mobility in disadvantaged communities through grants for public transit, walkability and more.

HIGH-SPEED RAIL AND TRAIN SYSTEMS

Strategic development of nationwide high-speed rail transforms mobility while boosting economic interconnectivity between regions. This 100-year vision modernizes intercity travel and public transport to an integrated network for the 21st century.

Here are some key focus areas for high-speed rail and train infrastructure in the US over the next 100 years:

- Construct dedicated bullet train corridors linking major mega-regions and metropolitan areas across the country to enable rapid, fuel-efficient travel. These include routes like California-to-Texas, Chicago-to-New York, etc.

- Upgrade existing Amtrak infrastructure for next-generation high speed trains by modernizing tracks, electrifying lines, and implementing signaling/safety upgrades to go up to 220+ mph where geography allows.

- Build out multi-modal transit hubs connecting high speed rail to local rail, light rail public transit networks to facilitate smooth last-mile connections.

- Establish public/private partnerships with railway technology providers to develop American-made trains, signaling equipment and safety systems for domestic routes. Cultivate associated R&D and manufacturing.

- Offer tax subsidies, land grants, and low interest loans to encourage dense walkable, transit-oriented development around stations across small towns and urban areas to maximize use.

- Implement commuter rail and S-Bahn like rapid transit lines around growing metro areas to serve mid-range mobility using high speed rail trunk route infrastructure.

AIRPORTS AND AIR TRAVEL

Strategic investments made today considering long-term air transportation needs stretching to the year 2100 and beyond lays the groundwork for sustaining US aviation dominance and mobility.

Here are some of the key things the US should focus on regarding airport and aviation infrastructure over the next 100 years:

- Construct additional super-capacity next-gen airports with flexibility for future expansion in major metro regions to meet project air traffic demand.

- Modernize the air traffic management system with satellite-based navigation, digital communications and advanced automation to enable more direct routing.

- Build higher-speed inter-airport rail connections so that door-to-door travel linking airports' arrival flight times for short haul routes under 500 miles.

- Establish renewable energy microgrids at airports offering storage and generation on-site to strengthen grid resilience during disruptions.

- Implement new modular terminal architectures using flexible layouts and prefabrication production to enable cost-effective expansion.

- Innovate passenger-friendly space like indoor urban farms, multi-modal transport lounges, and parks to enhance the airport experience over long dwell times.

- Cultivate biofuel-adapted aircraft and support infrastructure to utilize sustainable aviation fuels for reducing carbon emissions over decades.

PART 7
Energy

WHERE ARE WE NOW?

The US enjoys abundant indigenous energy resources but remains heavily carbon-intensive while also grappling with aging 20th-century infrastructure ill-suited to meeting 21st-century economic decarbonization and resilience priorities. Strategic reforms are needed.

THE CURRENT STATE OF US ENERGY

Strengths:

- Abundant domestic fossil fuel reserves (oil, gas, coal) enabling self-sufficiency

- World-leading renewable energy innovation ecosystem in solar, wind, batteries

- Declining reliance on imported energy driven by shale boom over last decade

- Plentiful farmland allowing growing production of biofuels as supplement

Weaknesses:

- Aging electricity transmission and distribution infrastructure prone to failures.

- High and volatile consumer costs due to variability in oil/gas markets.

- Energy policy uncertainty from frequent partisan conflicts hampers long-term investment.

- Renewables are still a small percentage of total supply requiring subsidies and favorable policies.

- Buildings, industry, and transportation remain heavily fossil fuel dependent.

- Greenhouse gas emissions near global highs per capita requiring systematic cuts.

WHAT DO WE NEED TO DO?

The decisions made today will reverberate for decades and determine the degree of US energy independence, sustainability, affordability and resilience over the next 100 years.

Here are some of the key things the US should focus on regarding energy infrastructure and policy over the next century:

- Continue expanding renewable energy portfolio—solar, wind, geothermal—with a goal of achieving 90% clean electricity by 2050 through subsidies, bonds, and construction incentives.

- Increase investment and incentives for next-gen nuclear power to provide stable baseline power supply as part of the mix along with renewables growth.

- Modernize and harden the aging energy grid infrastructure with a focus on resilience, smart grid technologies, local micro-grids, and transmission efficiency upgrades.

- Establish strategic petroleum reserve (SPR)-like national reserves of battery metals and critical energy minerals essential for the transition to give the US supply security.

- Enable two-way metering and decentralization of power generation without penalizing people who furnish electricity via solar panels or other means.

- Set stricter building energy efficiency standards each code cycle while incentivizing both new construction and deep retrofits of existing building stock to lower energy usage footprints.

- Increase funding for both fundamental energy research and pilot demonstrations of pre-commercial technologies with breakthrough potential in areas like fusion, batteries, bio-fuels, and geothermal.

PART 8

American Legal System

RULE OF LAW

The rule of law is essential to society for several reasons. In essence, the rule of law is crucial for the functioning of a just and democratic society, as it establishes the principles of accountability, just laws, open government, and accessible and impartial justice. It is widely recognized as a cornerstone of a fair and equitable society, ensuring that no one is above the law and that everyone is treated equally before it.

Here are some more specifics on why the Rule of Law is vital to our nation's long-term prospects:

1. Predictability and Stability: Rule of law establishes a clear framework of rules and principles that apply to everyone equally. This creates a predictable environment where individuals and businesses can function with confidence, knowing their rights and obligations. This predictability fosters stability and encourages long-term planning and investment.

2. Protection of Rights and Freedoms: The rule of law ensures the protection of fundamental rights and freedoms, including freedom of speech, assembly, and religion. It holds the government accountable and prevents it from overstepping its bounds or infringing on individual liberties. This protection creates a sense of security and promotes individual autonomy.

3. Fairness and Justice: The rule of law upholds the principle of equality before the law, meaning everyone is subject to the same rules and procedures, regardless of their social status, wealth, or political connections. This ensures fair and impartial treatment within the legal system and promotes a sense of justice for all.

4. Economic Prosperity: Societies with a strong rule of law tend to experience greater economic growth and development. Businesses thrive in environments where contracts are enforced, property rights are protected, and corruption is low. This attracts investment, fosters innovation, and ultimately benefits everyone in the society.

5. Conflict Resolution: The rule of law provides a peaceful and orderly mechanism for resolving disputes and conflicts. It promotes dialogue, compromise, and adherence to established legal procedures, preventing conflicts from escalating and contributing to social harmony.

6. Accountability and Transparency: The rule of law demands transparency and accountability from both the government and individuals. It ensures that laws are not arbitrary or biased and that those who break the law are held accountable, regardless of their position or influence. This promotes greater trust in institutions and strengthens the social fabric.

7. Long-Term Sustainability: While other forms of governance may offer stability in the short term, societies built on the rule of law tend to be more resilient and adaptable in the long run. They are better equipped to handle challenges, overcome crises, and evolve with time, laying the foundation for a sustainable and prosperous future.

HOW ARE WE DOING?

While the US has a robust legal system and a long-standing tradition of the rule of law, several factors have impacted its standing in global rankings:

1. Perceived Corruption: The perception of undue influence, lobbying, and money in politics, especially after decisions like Citizens United v. FEC, which allowed for increased corporate spending in political campaigns, can contribute to views of systemic corruption or undue influence.

2. Criminal Justice System Concerns: Issues like mass incarceration, the war on drugs, and reported racial biases in the justice system have drawn significant criticism. The US has one of the highest incarceration rates in the world, which can affect perceptions of the rule of law.

3. Civil Justice Concerns: The accessibility and affordability of civil justice is a concern for many in the US. Litigation can be costly and protracted, limiting access for many citizens.

4. Due Process Concerns: There have been concerns and criticisms related to due process, especially in the context of the war on terror, including issues related to Guantanamo Bay and the treatment of detainees.

5. Polarization and Trust: Political polarization can erode trust in institutions, including the legal system. If different groups perceive the legal system as biased or politicized, it can lower overall confidence in the rule of law.

6. Complex Regulatory Environment: The US has a complex legal and regulatory environment which can sometimes result in inefficiencies or perceived lack of clarity.

7. Rights and Policing: High-profile cases of police misconduct, use of force, and the subsequent public reactions and protests can affect perceptions of the rule of law.

WHAT CHANGES ARE NEEDED?

THE US SUPREME COURT

RADICAL IDEA #43: The US Supreme Court must act as a third branch of government as designed, not beholden to or at the direction of any US political party.

Why does the US Supreme Court so often rule strictly along political lines? A Supreme Court Justice's role is to interpret the law, not cast their vote aligned to the interests of the political party that appointed them. The frequent alignment of the US Supreme Court's rulings along political party lines raises questions about its independence and its ability to fulfill its constitutional role. It is essential to address these concerns to uphold the Court's integrity and its responsibility as the guardian and interpreter of the Constitution.

The US Supreme Court must perform its role as defined in the US Constitution. A pillar of American democracy rests upon the Supreme Court's ability to render objective judgments bounded by law and constitutional precedent, not ideological interests or partisan loyalty. Eroding public trust in the court's impartiality risks delegitimizing its essential role to balance competing visions democratically for the preservation of the republic.

While reasonable minds can respectfully disagree on interpretations aligned to judicial philosophy, justices ideally serve to uphold collective wisdom far beyond temporary political winds.

Frequent narrow rulings that ignore substantial consensus and standards established across decades reverberate instability carrying unintended consequences.

The integrity of the Supreme Court is paramount, and its credibility hinges on adherence to the Constitution. It's essential for the Court to uphold its constitutional mandate and for Justices to demonstrate that their decisions are grounded in legal reasoning, not partisanship. This is crucial for maintaining public trust in the nation's highest court and ensuring the separation of powers that is the bedrock of American democracy.

THE LOWER FEDERAL COURTS

RADICAL IDEA #44: Make judicial impartiality cool again at all levels.

The integrity of the lower federal courts in the United States is contingent upon their commitment to judicial independence and good faith action. These courts are expected to render decisions based on law and constitutional principles, rather than partisan directives. During the 2016 election cycle and subsequent presidency, the appointment of conservative judges emerged as a key priority for many of President Trump's supporters. Simultaneously, Senate Majority Leader Mitch McConnell was notably active in facilitating the confirmation of judges with conservative leanings to various levels of the federal judiciary. This strategy aimed to shape the judicial landscape, reflecting a broader political objective to influence the interpretation and application of the law for years to come.

At all levels, an impartial judiciary independent of partisan influence stands vital to equitable democracy and just rule of law. While judges hold varying philosophies, fulfilling their duties in good faith requires applying the law fairly to facts at hand, not as instruments of political actors.

Eroding public trust in freedom from bias risks delegitimizing the courts' essential role to balance competing visions democratically. Narrow rulings appearing politically motivated reverberate instability with unintended consequences.

By selecting judicious legal experts focused on principles over personalities, the promise of equal justice under law persists for generations. While reasoned disagreement is expected, consistency, integrity, and respect for precedents established across decades must outweigh partisan loyalty.

IMPROVING THE ENTIRE US LEGAL SYSTEM

Looking at the entire system, improving the rule of law and the legal system in the United States at every level requires a multifaceted and comprehensive approach. It involves addressing challenges and shortcomings in various aspects of the legal system, from local to federal levels. Here are several key areas and actions that can contribute to such improvement:

1. Judicial Independence and Accountability:

- Strengthen safeguards for judicial independence to ensure judges can make decisions based on the law without political pressure.

- Establish effective mechanisms for judicial accountability and ethical oversight to maintain public trust.

2. Access to Justice:

- Increase funding for legal aid programs and pro bono services to make legal representation more accessible to low-income individuals.

- Simplify legal procedures and provide self-help resources to assist individuals navigating the legal system without an attorney.

3. Criminal Justice Reform:

- Implement comprehensive criminal justice reform measures to address issues such as mass incarceration, mandatory minimum sentences, and racial disparities.

- Invest in rehabilitation and reentry programs to reduce recidivism.

4. Police Reform and Accountability:

- Promote community policing models and de-escalation training for law enforcement.

- Establish effective civilian oversight mechanisms and independent review boards to investigate allegations of police misconduct.

5. Legal Education and Training:

- Support ongoing education and training for legal professionals to ensure they are well-informed about current laws and best practices.

- Promote diversity in the legal profession to reflect the demographics of the population.

6. Transparency and Accountability:

- Enhance transparency in government operations, including public access to government records and meetings.

- Strengthen mechanisms for oversight and accountability of government agencies and officials.

7. Electoral and Political Reform:

- Address campaign finance reform to reduce the influence of money in politics.

- Address gerrymandering and support nonpartisan redistricting processes.

- Promote and protect the right to vote and ensure fair and accessible elections.

8. Technology and Innovation:

- Invest in technology upgrades and digitalization of legal processes to improve efficiency and accessibility.

- Ensure the ethical and responsible use of technology, such as AI and data analytics, in the legal system.

9. Public Education and Awareness:

- Promote civic education and legal literacy to ensure that citizens understand their rights and responsibilities under the law.

- Encourage public participation in legal and policy discussions.

10. International Engagement:

- Collaborate with international organizations and counterparts to exchange best practices and ideas for improving the rule of law.

11. Community and Stakeholder Engagement:

- Engage with local communities and stakeholders to identify and address specific legal system challenges and needs.

12. Continuous Assessment and Reform:

- Regularly assess the legal system's performance, identify
areas for improvement, and implement reforms as needed.

PART 9

Social Fabric of America

America's social fabric is complex and dynamic, woven from diverse threads of identity, values, and experiences. While it boasts considerable strength and vibrancy, it also faces a number of challenges and tensions that threaten its cohesion.

Among these challenges, a growing sense of hopelessness grips millions of US citizens, affecting people of all ages, particularly the younger generation. This pervasive hopelessness has led to a sense of disillusionment, with many questioning the prospects of a brighter future. This disillusionment has manifested in troubling ways, such as widespread drug abuse, reckless behaviors, and inadequate financial preparations for the uncertain road ahead.

AREAS OF CONCERN

Political Polarization

- Partisan divides have deepened, leading to acrimonious debates, distrust of opposing viewpoints, and a sense of national disunity. This polarization can hinder effective governance and erode trust in democratic institutions.

Socioeconomic Inequality

- The gap between the rich and the poor continues to widen, creating divisions based on economic opportunity, access to resources, and quality of life. This inequality can fuel resentment, hinder social mobility, and limit the potential of a large segment of the population.

Racial and Ethnic Tensions

- Despite progress made in civil rights, racial and ethnic disparities persist in areas like education, employment, healthcare, and criminal justice. This can lead to social unrest, discrimination, and a sense of exclusion for marginalized communities.

Cultural Clashes

- Diversity can be a source of strength, but competing values and lifestyles can also lead to misunderstandings, conflicts, and a sense of cultural fragmentation. This can make it difficult to forge a shared national identity and sense of purpose.

Erosion of Civic Engagement

- Declining rates of voter participation, volunteering, and community involvement weaken the bonds that hold society together. This can lead to apathy, a sense of voicelessness, and a decreased willingness to contribute to the common good.

Misinformation and Disinformation

- The rise of social media and the proliferation of fake news and misinformation can spread distrust, confusion, and animosity. This can undermine social cohesion, fuel extremism, and make it harder to reach common ground on important issues.

Mental Health and Social Disconnection

- Rising rates of anxiety, depression, and loneliness contribute to social isolation and a sense of disconnection from others. This can lead to increased conflict, decreased empathy, and a weakened sense of community.

It's important to note that these challenges are complex and multifaceted, with roots in history, economics, policy, and cultural shifts. Addressing them effectively will require sustained efforts across various sectors.

MAKE KEY SOCIAL ISSUE DECISIONS AT THE RIGHT LEVEL

RADICAL IDEA #45: Let states handle states' matters.

For many of our most contentious social issues, let's get back to the basics: let states handle states' issues. This will solve a lot and remove several sources of tension at the national level. What do I mean by that?

Many social issues in America right now—abortion, gay rights, gender issues, and much more—boil down to issues that are intended to be settled or resolved by communities, not at the federal level. If California, or cities in California, want something different from the Midwest, that is fine and part of the original design. Live and let live.

The United States Constitution divides powers between the federal government and the state governments. The federal government has certain powers that are specifically enumerated in the Constitution, such as the power to regulate commerce, declare war, and raise an army. The states have all other powers, and they are also responsible for enforcing federal laws within their borders.

The Constitution purposefully leaves many matters to state and local discretion rather than federal control. Broadly, areas intended to be reserved for state and community governance include the following:

- **Public Health, Safety, and Morals:** States have police powers over local laws and regulations covering these areas.

- **Education:** The Constitution does not mention education, leaving it to states and communities.

- **Local Government and Municipality Functions:** Zoning, sanitation, transportation, and local services are under local civilian control.

- **Professional Licensure:** Requirements for certain professions are determined at the state level.

- **Insurance Regulation:** States oversee insurance industry and policies.

- **Conduct of Elections/Voting:** State and local officials run elections, not the federal government.

- **Intrastate Commerce:** States can set laws governing commerce only within state borders.

- **Family Law:** Laws around marriage, divorce, adoption handled by states.

The Tenth Amendment in the US Constitution affirms powers not delegated to the US government are reserved for states and the public. The founders sought to prevent excessive federal overreach into local affairs.

There are also a number of topics that are considered to be shared responsibilities between the federal government and the state governments. These include environmental protection, public health, and welfare.

Welfare is a topic that has been the subject of much debate in recent years. The federal government provides funding for welfare programs, but the states are responsible for administering these programs. There have been calls for the federal government to take a more active role in welfare reform, but there is also concern that this would lead to an overreach of federal power.

I am deferring to the states and communities for most of these contentious social issues, but I felt come commentary was necessary for a handful of specific, understandably contentious issues. Those follow.

GUN RIGHTS

RADICAL IDEA #46: Strongly support Second Amendment gun rights, but with smart guardrails.

The right to bear arms is enshrined in the US Constitution. However, that doesn't mean we can all have tanks and nuclear submarines. Striking a fair and constitutional balance in gun regulation invites a spectrum of ethical and practical considerations. Certain measures can safeguard public safety while preserving our Constitutional rights to self-defense and recreational use of firearms.

Proposals that may garner broader agreement include the following:

- Comprehensive universal background checks required for all firearm sales to deter transfers to high-risk individuals. This would still allow ownership broadly.

- Mandated safety training demonstration prior to purchases to ensure basic handling proficiency and care, thus mitigating accidents without limiting the rights of responsible owners.

- Temporary restraining orders enabling temporary firearm restrictions from those deemed in imminent risk of harming themselves or others, focused only on definitive near-term risks.

- Rigorously enforced accountability for firearms owners, including mandatory reporting of theft coupled with penalties for failure to properly secure weapons, which disincentivizes black market trafficking.

THE US HEALTHCARE SYSTEM

RADICAL IDEA #47: Overhaul the US healthcare system, with an eye toward improving outcomes while driving cost out.

The US healthcare system will need a major overhaul to support the aging population in the near term as well as the needs of generations of Americans in the long-term.

This will be a challenge for several reasons, including funding. Medicare and Medicaid aren't adequately funded, maybe to a worse degree than the Social Security system.

What does the US healthcare system need to look like for the next 100 years and beyond? Here's what needs to happen.

- **Financial Sustainability:** Finding a balance between providing comprehensive coverage and ensuring long-term affordability through progressive taxation, employer contributions, and cost-effective care models.

- **Universal Coverage:** Ensuring all citizens have access to affordable, quality healthcare, regardless of income or employment status. This could involve expanding existing programs like Medicare or implementing a single-payer system.

- **Focus on Prevention and Primary Care:** Emphasizing preventive measures, wellness checks, and accessible primary care services to manage chronic conditions, reduce future healthcare costs, and improve overall health outcomes.

- **Innovation and Technology Adoption:** Encouraging and integrating telemedicine, wearable health trackers, and AI-powered diagnostics to improve access, personalize care, and reduce costs.

- **Equity and Access:** Addressing disparities in healthcare access and outcomes for vulnerable populations based on race, ethnicity, income, and geographic location. This may involve targeted interventions, culturally competent care, and rural healthcare initiatives.

- **Patient-Centered Care:** Empowering patients with information, choice, and control over their healthcare decisions, promoting shared decision-making with healthcare providers.

- **Focus on Value and Quality:** Shifting from payment models based on quantity of care to those rewarding quality outcomes, cost-effectiveness, and patient satisfaction.

- **Workforce Development and Retention:** Investing in training and retaining healthcare professionals, including primary care physicians, nurses, and mental health specialists, to address potential shortages and ensure a skilled workforce.

- **Public/Private Partnerships:** Collaborating with public and private stakeholders, including insurers, providers, and pharmaceutical companies, to achieve shared goals like affordability, innovation, and improved access.

IMMIGRATION

RADICAL IDEA #48: Convert the US immigration system from a major failure into a vital asset.

People are vital to our nation's long-term plans. However, we need the right people in sufficient numbers. By "right", I mean people with skills aligned to our long-term plans and economic needs. America needs to turn its immigration system into an asset, aligned to support the nation's long-term plans.

That isn't the system we have currently.

RADICAL IDEA #49: Pause immigration until we can figure out how best to fix the system long-term.

RADICAL IDEA #50: While the immigration process is paused, increase resources to clear the backlog.

The US immigration system is currently broken—badly broken. The problem is so bad that we need to immediately halt the process and increase resources for processing applications and hire more immigration judges to clear the current backlog.

The Trump administration proposed the construction of a border wall and the implementation of more stringent immigration controls as solutions to unauthorized immigration. While border states and sanctuary cities alike feel the pressures of current policies, any overhaul of the immigration system must balance legality with humanity. The new immigration system also needs to help enable execution of our nation's long-term strategies. We need people to innovate, create new businesses, as well as to do things like build our infrastructure and produce the food we all need.

The US should not continue to allow illegal immigrants to displace people applying through legal process. There's a massive backlog in visa applications and immigration court cases, leading to years of waiting for many individuals. There is a huge problem with people falsely claiming asylum. The US should suspend or pause asylum process until we have the improved system in place and ready to function.

The new, overhauled immigration system should adequately address the economic needs of the country in a manner aligned with the country's long-term plans.

RADICAL IDEA #51: Overhaul the US immigration system into a long-term plan aligned, merit-based system.

For leading practices around merit-based national immigration systems, we can look to Canada, Singapore, Australia, the UK, and Germany. We can pull in the best elements from those solutions that might work for the US, but the US's new immigration system must be kept aligned with its long-term strategic plans as a nation. Again, the US needs to encourage people with the right skills in the right numbers to our shores. We also need to have robust support for family unification for those folks who meet those standards. That approach will form the basis of the best immigration system the world has ever known.

PART 10

America's Place in the World

RADICAL IDEA #52: Foreign policy is often choices between two or more bad options.

It's impossible to please everyone in US foreign policy. There's no magic bullet. In fact, the decisions involved are often between two or more bad options. However, the United States is a global power, and as a force for good in the world, it needs to lead from the front.

American leadership, though not always welcome, often plays a crucial role in maintaining stability and advancing democratic values. This mantle of responsibility comes with a heavy cost, though, demanding constant strategic judgment and a willingness to grapple with moral dilemmas.

At a high level, an overarching US foreign policy strategy for the next century should generally entail:

- **Relationships Based on Respect:** Strengthening relationships with democratic allies and strategic partners through bilateral trade, shared security initiatives, technological research collaboration and defend democratic values globally.

- **Soft Power and Public Diplomacy:** Leveraging soft power through cultural influence, public diplomacy, and international broadcasting to project a positive image of the US globally.

- **Promoting Global Stability:** The US should continue to play a leading role in maintaining global peace and stability through diplomacy, alliances, and multilateral institutions. Responsibly competing with rival authoritarian regimes by asserting credibility, leadership, and deterrence without escalating risky direct confrontation where avoidable. Manage tensions soberly.

- **Military Innovation and Defense:** Ensuring military capabilities are advanced and proportionate to the challenges of the new era without engaging in arms races or overextension.

- **Space Policy:** Positioning the US as a leader in space exploration, security, and the developing space economy.

- **Multipolar Landscape:** Recognizing the shift from a unipolar world towards a multipolar one with rising powers like China, India, and Russia, shaping alliances and strategies accordingly. Shaping new alliances and multilateral agreements across Latin America, Africa, and Southeast Asia as power dynamics shift over the next 50–100 years to secure interests.

- **Diplomacy**: Serving as mediators and facilitators reducing conflicts and building bridges to deescalate and unite, avoiding spreading democracy primarily through military means which proves costly. Diplomacy first.

- **Counter Terrorism and Non-Proliferation:** Continuing efforts to combat terrorism and prevent the spread of weapons of mass destruction are essential for global security.

- **Lead from the Front:** Maintaining global leadership in technological innovation, economic ingenuity, higher education, pursuing sustainable abundance over zero-sum relative gains. Inspire by example.

- **Educational and Cultural Exchanges:** Encouraging educational and cultural exchanges can foster mutual understanding and build networks of future leaders with a favorable view of the US.

- **Partnerships:** Championing international cooperation around climate change policy, nuclear proliferation curbs, global public health and disaster response initiatives showing US commitment to advancing developing regions through partnerships.

- **Energy Security and Transition:** Leading in the transition to renewable energy sources and ensuring energy security through diversification.

CHINA

RADICAL IDEA #53: China is playing to win. So should we.

China's meteoric rise over the past four decades has been unparalleled in modern history. Since the 1980s, China has transformed from a largely agrarian economy to the world's manufacturing powerhouse. This economic boom has funded the development of a sophisticated economy and a formidable military presence, encompassing advancements in space, cyber capabilities, and traditional military arenas on land, sea, and air. The Chinese military has evolved far beyond its historical "peasant army" roots.

RADICAL IDEA #54: China wants to challenge the US worldwide, both economically and militarily by mid-century. Account for this strategically.

China's ambition doesn't stop at regional dominance. China aspires to surpass the United States' military prowess in East Asia within the next decade or two. Their strategic goal extends to diminishing US influence in East Asian politics and eventually contesting the US on the global stage, both economically and militarily, by the mid-21st century.

However, the objective is not to engage in a great power war. History has taught us the devastating impact of such conflicts in WWI and WWII. Instead, China seems to seek a position of strength that ensures peace through deterrence, all while avoiding direct armed confrontation with the United States.

RADICAL IDEA #55: Everyone loses in a military fight between the US and China.

Despite it not being the sole point of contention between China and the US, Taiwan sits at a critical geopolitical crossroads. A military conflict between the US and China would be catastrophic, not just for the nations involved, but for the entire world. War games consistently highlight the devastating potential losses, with even "victories" coming at immense human and economic cost.

Chinese President Xi Jinping has recently moved up his self-imposed deadline for achieving "unification" with Taiwan to 2027. While China currently lacks the full military capability for a full-scale invasion, its rapid advancements raise serious concerns.

The consequences of a US/China conflict extend far beyond the battlefield. Global trade would be disrupted, triggering economic collapse. Environmental damage from potential nuclear fallout or widespread destruction would be immense. Millions of lives would be lost, both in combat and due to secondary effects like famine and disease.

NORTH KOREA

RADICAL IDEA #56: Rethink the US's treatment of North Korea.

I want to see North Korea be as happy and prosperous as its neighbors, China and South Korea. My dream for North Korea's prosperity being comparable to that of its neighbors is currently just that, an aspiration. That isn't the trajectory the country is on right now.

Instead, our attention needs to be on the hypothetical scenario of a North Korean invasion of South Korea. Such action would lead to the catastrophic destruction of Seoul and immense loss of life. In such a regrettable event, there would be an undeniable need for significant political change in North Korea. The Kim regime's leadership would likely be untenable, and the transformation of North Korea's governmental structure would become imperative. This change, while necessary, should ideally occur without negatively impacting neighboring China, maintaining regional stability.

In the aftermath of such a transformative event, there is a possibility for North Korea to rebuild and prosper. With the right international support and internal reforms, the North Korean people could potentially experience a renaissance similar to South Korea's post-war economic miracle. This would require extensive international cooperation, investment, and a commitment to peace and development, allowing North Korea to integrate successfully into the global community.

ISRAEL

RADICAL IDEA #57: Israel is a strong, natural ally for the US for many reasons, but that support might erode over time.

Aligned with our 10 Guiding Principles in this book, US policy should show support and genuine respect for everyone in the region, not just the Israelis.

However, challenges exist.

RADICAL IDEA #58: There won't be a peaceful solution to the Israel/ Palestine conflict anytime soon.

The pursuit of peace in the Israeli/Palestinian conflict is hindered by the all-or-nothing stances of some leaders and extreme factions on both sides. The unfortunate reality is that these hardline positions often obstruct the path to a peaceful resolution, despite the potential for peaceful coexistence due to the cultural and historical commonalities among Arabs, Israelis, and Western nations. It's a shame since the Arabs and Israelis (as well as the US and much of the Europe) are natural cultural allies.

Regarding hypothetical scenarios of extreme violence, such as a large-scale attack by one side, it's important to advocate for responses that are proportional, targeted, and in accordance with international law and human rights standards. Advocating for widespread retribution, especially against civilians or family members, is not in line with these principles and does not contribute to a lasting solution.

For Israel, is killing every member of the extremist factions and their families the right answer? Some hardliners feel that is what works best as a deterrent. However, those extreme measures also make enemies of generations of Palestinians. The same argument works the other direction when Palestinian extremists kill Israelis. The cycle of hatred goes on and on.

The core of the conflict, deeply rooted in historical and religious differences, might indeed take generations to fully address. However, immediate safety and coexistence depend on both sides making significant cultural shifts towards mutual understanding and compromise.

RADICAL IDEA #59: A peaceful resolution of the Israeli/Palestinian problem isn't possible until the extreme right positions on both sides erode away over time.

Ultimately, lasting peace will require eroding the extreme positions of both sides that currently impede progress. This is a complex and challenging process, necessitating patience, diplomacy, and a commitment to peace from all involved parties. The 10 Guidelines in this book form the basis for an individual belief system that—once it is the prevalent belief system in a society—might just provide the cultural foundation needed to resolve this centuries-old conflict.

RADICAL IDEA #60: Support in the US for Israel might trend down in coming years.

Support for Israel across the US population isn't guaranteed forever. In fact, studies show that older generations of Americans tend to think of Israel more favorably than do younger generations. During their lifetimes, younger Americans have mostly been exposed to news of Israel's aggression and settlements, and support of Israel among those groups measures significantly lower. There is considerably more support and sympathy for Palestine among younger generations of Americans.

RADICAL IDEA #61: The current political trend in Israel is increasingly more to the right.

The current political trend in Israel is increasingly moving toward the right, with the current government and a growing number of young Israelis supporting right-wing parties and politicians. This shift is influenced by concerns about peace and security, the success of right-wing parties in promoting an ethnonationalist narrative, and historical events. As a result, the support for a two-state solution has declined significantly, with only a minority of Israeli Jews and Palestinians backing this approach. The far-right government in Israel has already begun implementing policies aligned with its agenda, such as proposed changes to the judicial system and plans to annex the occupied West Bank. This trend has raised concerns about the potential impact on the Israeli/Palestinian conflict and the rights of Palestinians.

The shift towards the right in Israeli politics has been attributed to various factors, including generational differences, security concerns, and the influence of right-wing parties and politicians. The decline in support for a two-state solution and the implementation of far-right policies by the Israeli government have significant implications for the future of the region and the prospects for peace between Israelis and Palestinians.

RADICAL IDEA #62: The Palestinians need a sense hope and a bright future for themselves and their families.

Currently, many Palestinians face a sense of hopelessness regarding their future, particularly in economic terms. However, envisioning a thriving economic landscape for Palestine involves recognizing its potential in various sectors. With the right support and opportunities, Palestine could develop a vibrant economy based on its unique strengths.

Let's dream about what Palestine's possible future could be together:

Agriculture: Leveraging its rich agricultural land, Palestine could enhance its production and export of olives, fruits, and vegetables, fostering a robust agribusiness sector.

Tourism: The rich historical and cultural heritage of Palestine, including significant religious sites, offers immense potential for developing a sustainable tourism industry that could attract visitors from around the world.

Technology and Entrepreneurship: Investing in education and technology infrastructure could pave the way for a thriving tech sector, encouraging innovation and attracting international investment.

Crafts and Manufacturing: Palestine has a rich tradition in crafts and manufacturing, which could be modernized and expanded, creating both local and export opportunities.

Renewable Energy: With its geographic location, Palestine could explore renewable energy sources, such as solar energy, contributing to both its energy independence and the global green economy.

Education and Human Capital: Investing in education and vocational training can create a skilled workforce capable of driving economic growth and innovation.

International Trade and Investment: Encouraging international trade and attracting foreign direct investment can help integrate the Palestinian economy into the global market.

IRAN

RADICAL IDEA #63: Rethink the US's treatment of Iran.

Similar to my policy proposal on North Korea, our disagreement with Iran is more with the current ruling regime than the Iranian people themselves. The US and Iran are natural cultural allies in many ways. There exists a potential for a mutually beneficial alliance between the US and Iran, grounded in shared historical and cultural ties that predate current tensions.

It is a stark reality that the use of nuclear weapons by any nation, including Iran, would trigger severe global consequences. Therefore, nuclear proliferation in Iran is a concern for international peace and security, and robust diplomatic efforts are necessary to prevent such an outcome.

The Middle East's stability is crucial for the global economy, given its significant role in the supply of hydrocarbons. Disruptions in this region could have dire repercussions on international energy markets and economic stability worldwide.

THE SUNNI/SHIA SPLIT

Understanding the Sunni/Shia split is also essential for crafting informed and nuanced US foreign policy. This sectarian divide has deep historical roots and influences the region's geopolitics, shaping alliances, conflicts, and power dynamics. Iran is primarily Shia and leads on one side, and Saudi Arabia is primarily Sunni and leads the other side in the region.

The Sunni/Shia split originated from a dispute over Islamic leadership succession following the death of the Prophet Muhammed in 632 AD. While both branches share fundamental beliefs and practices of Islam, differences emerged in their historical interpretation of leadership:

Sunnis believed the successor or caliph should be democratically chosen from the Muslim community based on merits.

Shias (shortened from "*Shiat Ali*" meaning "Party of Ali") favored hereditary succession belonging to Ali, the cousin and son-in-law of Muhammed, and his authorized descendants.

Over time, theological and political disputes fueled tensions as competing caliphates emerged. Sunni caliphates eventually consolidated control over the majority Islamic population. The Shia denomination also spread over time, becoming dominant in some regions like Iran.

Today, Sunnis comprise about 85–90% of Muslims globally while Shias make up 10–15%. Both share core foundations of Islamic faith alongside differences in certain spiritual practices, ritual traditions, and religious leadership authority. Geopolitical disputes frequently exploit these sectarian divides. However, their historical origins trace to early disagreements over rightful leadership succession.

From the US foreign policy standpoint, maintaining the flow of hydrocarbons from the Middle East is a strategic priority. Disruptions due to conflict would have catastrophic implications, not just for the region, but globally.

RUSSIA

RADICAL IDEA #64: Seek better relations with Russia while simultaneously defending every inch of NATO territory.

The US policy towards Russia should be multifaceted, balancing firm deterrence with avenues for dialogue and cooperation where possible.

The US's commitment to NATO is a cornerstone of this policy. The alliance serves not only as a collective defense mechanism but also as a platform for maintaining European security and peace. It is imperative that the US continues to uphold the principle of collective defense as enshrined in Article 5 of the NATO treaty, which states that an attack on one is an attack on all. This unwavering commitment acts as a powerful deterrent against aggression and ensures the integrity of member states' sovereignty.

In addition to a strong defense posture, the US must remain vigilant and resilient against threats to its security and way of life. This includes safeguarding democratic institutions, critical infrastructure, and the cyberspace against subversion, espionage, and attack.

However, defense and deterrence should be complemented by strategic dialogue. It is essential to keep diplomatic channels open with Russia to manage tensions, reduce the risk of conflict, and explore potential areas of mutual interest, such as arms control, counterterrorism, and regional stability.

The US should also continue to engage with its international partners and allies, reinforcing the rules-based international order. While the readiness to defend allies is paramount, the US must also exercise prudence in its alliances, ensuring that shared values, strategic interests, and the commitment to mutual defense are the basis of these partnerships.

Furthermore, the US should be prepared to respond proportionately to Russian actions that undermine international norms. This includes imposing economic sanctions in response to cyberattacks, election interference, and military aggression, as well as offering diplomatic and economic support to nations that may be vulnerable to Russian pressure or destabilization efforts.

Lastly, cultural and academic exchanges could serve as soft power tools to foster better mutual understanding between the peoples of Russia and the United States, potentially laying the groundwork for improved relations in the long term.

TRIBAL SOCIETIES

As for tribal societies, they are free to govern themselves as they see fit. From a US foreign policy perspective, we cannot force democracy or any other system of government on people who don't want it. The principle of self-determination is paramount. They have the sovereign right to choose their own form of governance. The US foreign policy approach acknowledges that while democracy is cherished domestically, it may not be the desired or optimal system for all nations and cultures.

In some regions with deep-seated tribal or historical divisions, strong centralized authority (normally a dictator backed by an army) has, at times, provided a semblance of stability. However, this is not an endorsement of autocracy. US foreign policy should encourage governance that ultimately serves the people's welfare and aligns with broader global interests, promoting human rights and sustainable development.

It's important to recognize that the aspirations for governance vary across the globe. The aim of US foreign policy should be to support the advancement of societies in a manner that respects their cultural contexts and political choices, without imposing a one-size-fits-all model. This approach encourages a more nuanced and pragmatic engagement with the international community.

RADICAL IDEA #65: Conflict is sometimes necessary.

Conflict is sometimes necessary. We don't want war. We want peace, and commerce, and mutual prosperity. However, if provoked or antagonized, we must be able to react decisively.

PART 11

Our Future

A FEW PARTING THOUGHTS

As I began this book by saying, as a nation, we are too focused on the short-term. Taking care of present concerns is important, but we also need to have a long-term roadmap for success for the country. We need to prioritize how we apply our limited resources. We need to have long-term strategies and execute those strategies competently and efficiently. These are non-negotiable steps the US must take if it is to continue to prosper and thrive in the future.

Second, the debt level of the US is a serious strategic vulnerability. One of the gravest challenges we face is the burgeoning national debt. It is acceptable for a country to incur a debt in certain cases, but that debt cannot continue forever and grow without limits. This vulnerability, if not addressed, has the potential to precipitate a decline of the US, fundamentally altering the nation as we know it. While the economic hurdles before us are formidable, there is still a window of opportunity to rectify our course—an opportunity that is not indefinite. We need to act.

Third, since the conclusion of World War II, the US has enjoyed a unique advantage due to the dollar's status as the primary reserve currency globally. However, this privileged position is under threat and may be relinquished. The repercussions of losing the dollar's hegemony could be profound, and we must be ready for such a possibility.

To address the undercurrent of animosity and tribalism that fosters global hostility, this book presents 10 Guiding Principles. These principles are designed not just as a beacon for the United States, but as a universal framework to foster mutual respect and understanding across cultures. They offer a pathway, starting at the individual level and, once applied by the millions, to mitigate conflicts that span from regional disputes like the Israeli/Palestinian tension, to international challenges such as Russian aggression in Ukraine, and the multifaceted adversities involving Iran. The offer a simple and understandable philosophical foundation for creating the roadmap that we need for future success.

Let's come together and get this done. With millions of Americans' heads all pointed in one productive direction, we can build the future that we all want and deserve.

Do it for yourself.

Do it for your family.

Do it for your community.

Do it for future generations.